WILLOW, WINE, MIRROR, MOON

Willow, Wine, Mirror, Moon

Women's Poems from Tang China

Translated from the Chinese
with an Introduction by

Jeanne Larsen

BOA Editions, Ltd. ❦ Rochester, NY ❦ 2005

Second Edition
2013

Publications by BOA Editions, Ltd.—
a not-for-profit corporation under section 501 (c) (3)
of the United States Internal Revenue Code—
are made possible with the assistance of grants from
the Literature Program of the New York State Council on the Arts;
the Literature Program of the National Endowment for the Arts;
the Sonia Raiziss Giop Charitable Foundation; the Lannan Foundation;
the Mary S. Mulligan Charitable Trust; the County of Monroe, NY;
the Rochester Area Community Foundation;
the Elizabeth F. Cheney Foundation; the Ames-Amzalak Memorial Trust
in memory of Henry Ames, Semon Amzalak and Dan Amzalak;
the Chadwick-Loher Foundation in honor of Charles Simic and Ray Gonzalez;
the Steeple-Jack Fund; the Chesonis Family Foundation,
as well as contributions from many individuals nationwide.

Cover Design: Prime8 Media
Cover Art: "Pink Peony 2" by Lucinda Storms, courtesy of the artist
Interior Design and Composition: Richard Foerster
Manufacturing: McNaughton & Gunn, Lithographers
BOA Logo: Mirko

Library of Congress Cataloging-in-Publication Data

Willow, wine, mirror, moon : women's poems from Tang China / translated with
notes and introduction by Jeanne Larsen.— 1st ed.
    p. cm. — (Lannan translations selection series)
  Includes bibliographical references.
  ISBN 978-1-929918-74-7 (pbk. : alk. paper) — ISBN 978-1-929918-73-9 (cloth : alk.
paper)
  1. Chinese poetry—Women authors—Translations into English. 2. Chinese
poetry—Tang dynasty, 618-907—Translations into English. I. Title: Women's
poems from Tang China. II. Larsen, Jeanne. III. Series.

PL2658.E3W52 2005
895.1'130809287—dc22

                          2005017455

BOA Editions, Ltd.
250 North Goodman Street, Suite 306
Rochester, NY 14607
www.boaeditions.org
A. Poulin, Jr., Founder (1938–1996)

for Tom Mesner

patient, witty feminist

with love

Contents

II

Women of the Household

III
Courtesans and Entertainers

IV
Women of Religion

Introduction

Poems from the Tang dynasty (618–907) have been at work in the Chinese poetry of every subsequent age and on a remarkable amount of Western writing over the past hundred years. Yet in 1667, a much-admired poet named Wang Duanshu had this to say in the preface to her copious anthology of poems by women, almost all from her own day or not long before: "It particularly pains me to find that so little of the poetry of the women of the past survives, and that what does remain is the work of so few authors."

This book represents the traces of 44 Tang women, 109 poems. Actually, the originals come from the Tang *era*—some were written in the interesting half-century or so after the dynasty's last emperor was deposed. But the cultural force of the empire called Great Tang was not extinguished with the end of one family's rule: it is reasonable to read work from the shifting patchwork of lesser states called the Five Dynasties and Ten Kingdoms as "Tang poetry." Long-term changes were underway, in sensibilities and poetic form, but poets of those years looked on themselves as heirs to Tang literary traditions.

Silenced people find ways to reach into the world around them. They can defy a social rule or make clever use of one. They can object obliquely to how things are. Their voices do sometimes enter history's register. Not all female Tang subjects were denied the boon of reading, even though a few of these poems may have been created by women dependant on no more than a good mind and a good ear.

In China (as elsewhere) in the seventh, eighth, ninth and tenth centuries (among others), being female reduced a person's chance of experiencing the satisfactions of making poems. It also limited who read the poetry she might have written down and affected the likelihood of its preservation. Conventional thinking regarding gender restricted the topics and attitudes a female poet might adopt. This last had pros and cons: Women poets found their ways to deal with such conventions—from embracing, to evading, to giving them transforming twists.

Substantial numbers of women's poems were lost during the Tang, as after and before; there are reports of collections reduced to a fraction, or vanished entirely. But Chinese traditions of regard for poetry and the historical record meant that manuscripts were copied out for friends, anthologists safeguarded favorites, and samplings were passed on privately within families. Men of means could be intrigued or titillated by women bold enough to write, even if they expected from their daughters-in-law not a word.

More than 2200 writers appear in the *Complete Tang Poems* (the enormous eighteenth-century anthology from which I've selected what is translated here). Well over a hundred of them were girls or women; the count would exceed 130 if we accepted the authenticity of every entry attributed to a female, excepting only ghosts, dream-figures, or the like. Considering that over eight centuries had passed when that flawed but monumental anthology was completed, considering the pressures toward feminine silence, we might be pleased there are so many.

The poets in this book lived out a diversity of social roles. Over the past seventeen years and more, I chose a mix of poems I thought I could carry over into English, poems with which I'd felt a crucial inner connection. (Wang Duanshu again: "I wished to make a selection that would be at once comprehensive and exquisite.") But how to arrange them? In the end, I followed other anthologists, including Wang; I've grouped the poets by their positions within their society.

Some themes recur throughout this volume—heartbreak, for example, or the mysteries and meanings of the natural world. But each section also reveals qualities congruent with its poets' characteristic life experiences, status-appropriate knowledge, and the varying expectations for their art. Imperial lady, homemaker, entertainer, nun—a writer's role in life apparently affected what we have of what she wrote.

Section I gathers empresses and other palace women, along with an aristocrat promoted to Princess for the sake of a political marriage. "Palace lady" (*gongnü* or *gongren*) is a wide-ranging term. Those taken into the household of an emperor or prince for the purposes of childbearing, sex, entertainment, and conspicuous consumption were precisely ranked; the *Complete Tang Poems* editors underscored this by positioning lower-level consorts such as Li Xunxian and Lady Pistilstamens well away from empresses and other highly-placed spouses. There were also capable women on the staff of the inner palaces whose main work was educational or administrative.

Some made the best of harem life and some endured it. At times during the Tang (there is no way to know how long, how often, or if it ever really stopped), a lively literary culture flourished in the imperial women's quarters, as in those of some short-lived kingdoms following the empire's breakup. A woman's poetic skill could be what brought her into a monarch's household in the first place. We may assume other palace ladies benefited from their leisure and made poems, although their works, like their faces, were kept unbesmirched by an outsider's gaze. In a few cases, women of the court won for themselves political positions that ensured their poetry would gain attention.

Tang women of the court wrote love plaints, and, like others, some celebrated the erotic force that was one of the few means of power at their command. They too could make blithe use of double-entendre to write of sex. They also made banquet poems exulting in the authority of China's only official female ruler (Wu Zhao *aka* Wu Zetian), compelling landscape lyrics, a poetic record of a royal progress, and a pair of poems that mingle guidance for an emperor with a prudent courtier's flattery.

Section II, Women of the Household, contains poems by writers of less elevated rank, some noble-born, some obscure. Most were wives in genteel households; poems attributed to maids and concubines have also been preserved under this category. (A concubine held a socially-recognized position, one closer to a servant than a formal wife. It might or might not have long tenure.) Other poets are identified as daughter, mother, granddaughter, sister, or niece of a better-known man.

In this section, "mainstream" (i.e., not gender-marked) topics show up, for instance, in Ms. Sun's lovely mood-piece on the emotional range of well-played music and in Zhang Wenji's exploration of the allegorical meaning of bamboo. In addition to such standard female-voice topics as romantic yearning and fear of losing love—the latter at times a quite pragmatic thing—some poems present advice for, or irritation at, a husband. A wife might also use her talent to help a man's career by providing poems he could claim as his own. There are, as well, poems written for other women, including Ms. Jiang's defiant statement of alcoholic bravado.

Too often, especially for women of the household, individual names are lost. Chinese names in this book are given in their proper order: first the family's, then—if it's known—the personal. When a poet has been recorded only under her husband's surname (as if Elizabeth Barrett Browning were known to us just as "Mrs. Browning"), I translate Zhang *furen* as "Madame Zhang." When she is listed, in the customary way, under the surname of her birth clan (as if the nineteenth-century English poet had been called lifelong "Mistress Barrett"), I render Zhao *shi* as "Ms. Zhao."

Questions of title are not at issue for the book's third section, work from poets who made their living as professional entertainers—successful courtesans, unhappy ones, singers enacting expressions of feminine fidelity for men far from home. Some won fame for their ways with words; their attentions, in the form of poem exchanges, were sought out by bright young men, and senior poets too. They lived as much by their wits and image-marketing as by sex appeal.

Tang courtesans held a status well above the prostitutes of their day. They knew themselves to be skilled artistes, like geisha in Japan. The same word, *ji*, applied to highly-schooled performers in troupes attached to the imperial household and to those whose companionship was available to men of lesser rank. This suggests that (even though they were divided into the emperor's "palace *ji*" and "officials' *ji*" or "commoners' *ji*," for instance) artistic ability, not sexual access, was the primary defining characteristic. In a society where male approval was often the name of the game, these women had appreciative audiences for their music, their dance, their poetry.

Still, courtesans' lives outside patriarchal households—yet within the patriarchal system—should not be idealized. They trafficked in more than glamour, stimulating companionship, and artistic gifts. Their sexual labor was available for hire, directly or indirectly. Their contracts, and so, their persons, could be sold or given away. And generally they did not receive the full profits for their work or even control who their clients were.

Courtesans in wine-houses, described as "fallen" and listed on government registers, had to remain in specified areas within their towns except for special occasions. Those attached to provincial military governments were in effect the governor's property and could be taken off to some remote new place when he was transferred—or be left behind for his successor. With age, all such women could only hope for the luck (in the form of a generous patron or a love-struck one) that might bring a position as a madam, a secure place as a musician and sexual partner in a kind man's household, or an entry into religious life.

Yet courtesans had opportunities. They modeled the manners of upper-class sophistication, an attractive quality for a young would-be official from a provincial home. They might form allegiances with up-and-coming members of the intellectual and political elite. The justly celebrated poet Xue Tao was one of the accomplished hostesses who nurtured male-to-male relationships that facilitated the running of the empire. Helping ambitious men network, softening up imperial inspectors, cultivating infatuations, filling an outsider in on the local dish: These could give courtesans a role in the careers of men in government. A savvy woman built a life on such possibilities. A curious one could turn the talk to history or poetry, and learn. One less fortunate might be taken up, then dropped.

Unlike women living with families, these poets were expected to display their talents. Doubtless, some guests of even the brightest courtesans accepted at face value the blandishments of those they thought of as admiring doxies: every age has its blindered fortunates. But other men, such as the poet Du Mu and the memoirist Sun Qi, did not mistake the absence of a standard (man's) education for lack of perceptiveness. They paid attention when a working girl uttered something thought-provoking or affecting or verbally dexterous.

Section IV, Women of Religion, includes the one extant poem by the only Tang Buddhist nun whose work survives, several poems by women who took Taoist holy orders, and an irresistible exchange between the spiritual seeker Lu Meiniang and her laywoman friend.

Those whose title is translated as "Ladies of the Tao" ("Female Capped-One" was another designation) came from all parts of society. Older women donned Taoist caps after decades in a different role. Younger ones found in this way of life an alternative to marriage. Girls might be placed in cloisters by penniless parents or in hopes of restoring their health.

As for Christian nuns in medieval Europe, life as a Taoist church-woman (or female priest or adept) could be a road to education and respect. Taoist convents—some 550 were on record in the mid-eighth century—served as centers for women's religious and intellectual endeavors. Some female scholars of the Tao maintained active social lives from a distinctive social space, receiving poems and visits from men of high position. The most disciplined undertook rigors (dietary abstinence, reclusion, visualization practices, exercises in breathing and body energetics) that imply they were quite serious about their spiritual goals.

Taoist women were sometimes romanticized, sometimes criticized, for their sexual behavior. In fact, this ranged from dedicated chastity to unlicensed prostitution to ritualized encounters with male divinities or mortal men. Male fantasies about these unmarried women mingled with age-old Taoist traditions treating sexual activity as a technology for spiritual development and physical well-being.

Religious themes and images run strong in this section, but they show up elsewhere, too. Nor did Taoist women restrict themselves from writing on other subjects. Yu Xuanji and Li Ye, the two from whom we have the most poems, left us some decidedly worldly work. Not surprising: It seems they led decidedly worldly lives.

In fact, in Tang society, all these niches for female subjects—court, household, entertainment world, cloister—were porous. Some women retired from a palace to the haven offered by a religious vocation, perhaps in their senior years or as a temporary expedient. A courtesan might do the same. Other entertainers were sold to aristocrats (or given as gifts), becoming concubines and "household artistes." Just as those who claimed the status of Lady of the Tao might work in the sex industry, so did abandoned concubines and refugees cut off from their old lives by war. Girls "of good family" could find themselves contracted to a wine-house out of financial necessity or as legal retribution for a relative's crime. Surely the poets among them all sometimes poured their hearts into their words and sometimes coolly performed the verbal postures expected in a given situation—say, a banquet or a farewell.

But who really wrote the poems translated here? There are, as the notes in the back of this book reveal, occasional uncertainties concerning authorship. A lady-in-waiting might ghostwrite for an empress. Someone hand-copying a manuscript or compiling an anthology might accidentally shift work from one courtesan to another or from a "Ms. Lu" to a "Ms. Hu." A poem passed down locally through the centuries might wind up credited to the best-known woman writer of the district, stuck to her corpus by charisma's glue.

Similar problems can apply to male poets of Tang times, though often there's a better chance of solving them. The *Complete Tang Poems* is far from definitive; there are instances of the same poem appearing twice, as two different writers' work. Scholars are working out more reliable texts and attributions, but mysteries (and, doubtless, errors) will remain.

Sometimes a woman's name may be attached to a male-authored poem. The flourishing, in medieval China, of female-persona poems by men increased the chances of slippage or misrepresentation. Beyond this, male Tang subjects were free to write about a noteworthy woman—including poetry they claimed she had composed—in romantic tales or collections of spicy anecdotes. Some such accounts were fact and some were fiction, surely. But later editors could gather up the verses without questioning the ascription.

Yet, a fictionalized narrative may preserve a nonfictional woman's actual poetry, however fanciful the prose context. And it's worth remembering that for more than a millennium's worth of readers, these poems have circulated with women's names attached. This had at least one important effect: Old poems by faux women (like those by real ones) helped give legitimacy to the great upwelling of literary work by women in the last two dynasties, the Ming and Qing, and beyond. The woman who "lives" only in a text can come to have a force not unlike that of her once-fleshly sister, who now lives . . . in a text.

Still, we may assume that almost all the poems in this book were written by whom they are said to have been written by, or by another woman rather like her. As the poet Luo Qilan stated in the preface to her late eighteenth-century anthology of poems and letters by contemporary women: "Let the derisive know there is no lack of talent among women; it is only that transmission of their work is twice as difficult as it is for men."

The poets represented in this book wrote out of the fertile store of Chinese poetry, from invigorating pop songs to richly literary verse.

They were not entirely deprived of role models. Some would have known about literary female aristocrats from preceding dynasties. There were also canonized folk songs understood to be women's words. And in the centuries just before the Tang, chanteuses in the pleasure quarters of South China offered lyrics that some literati imitated, and recorded. So Tang women had available to them artful channels for emotion and for construction of a voice—including channels marked as "womanly"—that had been dug by men and women both. These exemplars showed ways whereby they might, despite the silencing, have their say.

A writer named You Tong had this to say in his 1671 preface to another man's anthology of women's lyrics: "If these writings are lucky enough to be passed down to the world, then even after the author's rosy cheeks have turned to dust, later generations will still chant her pieces—will imagine how dangling tresses skimmed her brow as she moistened the tip of the brush with her lips and applied the ink." I'd put it this way: Reading poetry created despite restrictions on education and self-expression can open one more door to the enlargements of mind and spirit that aesthetic practice offers artist and audience alike. It can also raise blinds, revealing lives of resiliency, discernment, yearning, overt resistance and covert subversion, melancholy borne and joy discovered, desperation, strength.

—Jeanne Larsen

I
WOMEN OF THE COURT

Ms. Changsun, the Wende Empress (601–636)

Song: Wandering in Spring

The Imperial Park:
  apricot blossoms shine
  in the breaking day.
Rooms like orchids:
  a radiant girl
  moved by her feelings, by spring.
Above the well:
  new peaches steal
  from the flush of her face.
Beside the eaves:
  tender willows
  take after her light form.
Among the flowers:
  coming and going—watch
  dancing butterflies.
Up in the trees:
  now long, now
  brief—hear the orioles sing.
Within that grove:
  a retreat (what need
  to make inquiries far afield?)
long known to be free
  as currents of wind. No
  other is its like.

Empress Wu Zhao *aka* Wu Zetian (c. 627–705)

An Evening Banquet as the Year Begins, Wine Cups Floating Past

Now spring starts, the best
of seasons: a thousand

households throw their night gates
wide. Fresh flames

flare out from orchid
lanterns. A halo shines round

the new moon's bow.
This gift of wine is only

just enough. Let cup after cup
drift down the stream—skimp

and it's all a waste.
When my lords and envoys feel the rise

of sun-red libations' joy,
only then may they ride off, and buoyant

on the river Luo, become
again who they really are.

In the Stony-Torrents Mountains

Three pinnacles, ten caverns, and
a brightness to them ordered

by the mysteries On High; these jade
spires, these golden ranges, guard

the Imperial Home. They regulate
the dews and snow, no

pretty scene, no other feature
of this earth, their match. Crossed

by winds and crossed by rains, they flank
Our Capital. Ten-thousand-meter cliffs

hoard sun's hues, its gloss. Miles-long
and secret, ravines lie drenched

in cloaks of mist. But stop. Take joy
in feasting. Admire the creek-lover's

wisdom, the charity of hills. And then,
on jeweled saddles, as twilight

falls, above the roiling
dust, we'll fly away.

Shangguan Wan'er *aka* Shangguan Zhaorong (664–710)

Plaint: Her Beautiful Letters

when leaves first fall
into Cavegarden Lake   she
broods on him   a thousand
miles off and   more   dew
thickens   perfumed
quilts grow cold   the moon
slides close   and no
one's shadow fills her
bedroom's screen   she feels
like playing a love song
from the south   she's stuck
on sending letters to
the troubled north   in
those letters, nothing
gets said but this: how
she can't make
her peace with living
apart   for all this time

from Twenty-Five Poems upon Traveling to the Changning Princess's Floating Wine Cup Pond

#3

close-grown clusters   bamboo shadows
low moaning tones   the pine trees' sounds
no need to bother   with songs and pipes
it's all we need   this pleasure in the heart

#4

a long look up   toward one thatched shack
a gaze swept down   to high boughs' tips
daybreak's mist   drops by to pass the time
you wind and moon   with us, all's understood

#6

light-shot ripples   quiver, murmur
green-black forest   profound and dim
don't find fault   when footsteps linger
now we've climbed   to spice groves of the moon

#9

up the mountain   looking
far in a single
glance   I'm struck
by the long spring's
start   teams of horses
clog the boulevards   the fringe
of town   villagers
fill the city   settle
in   tumbling among
snowflakes   plum petals
sally forth   but
caught off-guard by
winds   the willows
won't open up   I'm only
sad because the sun
slants down   don't care
at all   that my wine cup
has gone dry

#11

just for a while   you've
traveled to this mountain
home   for love of it
you stay around   you don't
head back   your window
fills with sunset
clouds   till a clear
moon's light floods
in   doors open onto downwash
creeks   where white
mists hover   books
here can be shelved on
vines   and you could wear
a shaman's leafy
evergreen   this place is worth
the scramble up   look
outward   downward   feel
what it means   that
aureole   that
glory

#12

let loose   let loose to
move through cloud
and mist   in this sparse
solitude   it's natural
to rise above
the crowds   cleansed by
rushing water   what's
in my chest feels
pure   leaning on
this travel desk   I flee
that racket   those
miasmas   stones here
painted with the sheen
of moss   wind's shuttle
weaving ripples
on a stream   why prize
it so   this small house
in the hills?   only
for what lingers   scents
like moon-tree bark   white
orchises   a trace
of higher minds

#19

free for a while   to wander
where   hills give
what they give   and water's
wisdom runs   at
ease you get   a pine tree's
outlook   feel moon-trees'
heady spice   here's
word   for all who would
escape the
world   no need
to quest for paradise
away   beyond the sea

#21

beside this pond   I
think I'll test
my pen   lean on this
rock and—swept up—write
a poem   I'm ready
to play a song of creeks
and hills   but   no   it's
better to be one who
hears   and knows

Jiang Caiping (fl. 713, d. 756?)

Declining a Gift of Pearls

Two eyebrows, thin
  curved cassia
    leaves—long
      untouched
        by dye.

Dregs
  of make-up, mixed
    with tears, stain
      dark red raw
        silk.

Day wears down
  in the Palace of Gates
    Unending: left
      unwashed,
        uncombed.

What use are
  these precious
    pearls—
      comfort
        for desolation?

Yang Yuhuan, the Cherished Consort (717?–756)

For My Maidservant Zhang Yunrong, upon Seeing Her Dance

Gauzy
    sleeves
        release
their scent,
    a scent that
does not
    cease.   This
  red-flushed   lotus
whirls
    and   wavers
  among   autumnal
        mists.
  Cloudy
      wisps on a
  summit
    now!
  ripple in   the winds.
    And a delicate
pondside   willow
    starts
      to brush
  the   water, to
    sway.

The Yifen Princess (fl. 745)

Written on a Screen at Empty-Pond Courier Station

Sent out in marriage,
I leave my
Town and nation—
A parting harder
Than any in the past.

Imperial grace! I sorrow
At this long road,
Watch others on it
As they watch me,
And weep.

In desert border lands
Good looks wear
Away; near frontier
Shelters, kohl
And powder fade.

When will it break,
This mere woman's heart?
Some other day,
When I look
Homeward, toward Chang'an.

Song Ruoxin *aka* Song Ruoshen (d. 820?)

Teasing Lu Chang, a Bridesmaid from Down South

For the wedding, a mansion's
tower—twelve floors
upheld by a turquoise sky:

>   our nubile hen, her virile mate,
>   stand ready, face
>   to face on their nuptial tree.

But immortal Mistress Couple-up
brings heaven's decree
to the guards round the women's rooms:

>   *To this Han palace, here in the north,*
>   *don't let that drawling*
>   *country music in!*

Song Ruozhao (d. 825)

Poem Rhyming with One by His Majesty, Written as Ordered at a Banquet in Linde Palace with a Hundred Colleagues

All around the compass rose,   hands fold inside hanging sleeves:
solemnity and peace pervade   four gates, in four directions—
this is *nonaction*'s natural   result, and naught
to do with courtiers' exploits,   courtiers' feats.

To refine the intelligensia,   summon those who hide away.
To uphold the arts of war, destroy   the monstrous and the cruel.
When virtue's luminous, a glow   of youth burns bright.
Then grace and favor trickle down,   plenteous dew, thick rain.

Robes and caps of office   suit a royal feast;
proper rites and music   make court and monarch great.
Ten thousand harvests! Live forever!   This merits wine cups raised—
truly, may a thousand years   be no more than one.

Song Ruoxian (d. 835)

*Poem Rhyming with One by His Majesty,
Written at a Banquet in Linde Palace with a
Hundred Officials*

With proper obeisance, receive   commands from Heaven.
Unsullied times   sustain a saintly monarch.
One hears it in all quarters,   *he accepts reproof*;
from every region they come far,   to pay respects at court.

Here, where the scene enchants,   warblers begin to trill,
as spring draws to its end and days   grow longer yet.
This banquet created upon command: a flood of magnificence!
And all this sumptuous music: again it rings and sings.

You ancient capital cities,   who among you rivals this?
Even the ruins beyond the Fen—   not one can compare.
We wish our lord a long life, long   as the holy hills',
and happiness and blessings   without ending, without bounds.

Praiseworthy Consort Xu, Obedient and Sagely Queen Mother of Shu (c. 883–926) *and* Exemplary Consort Xu, Respectful and Sagely Dowager of Shu (d. 926)

from The Greenwall Pilgrimage Sequence

(four poems each, selected from a set of sixteen)

Darkmystic City Shrine

A thousand feet tall, these green crags catch
    rushing creeks between:

Climb up, look out, and realize
    how low, this sea of hills.

Cascades spill and pound gray-blue
    boulders into shards.

Tufts of grass we've cut across, and
    leafy peaks—the same.

Our footsteps stick to lichens, moss;
    a dragon bridge curves up, slick.

The sun's closed off by spreading mists;
    faint bird paths go astray.

Don't say of heaven's high-arched vault,
    no road can take you there.

These mountains are a stairway
    to clouds in deep blue sky.

(by the Praiseworthy Consort)

Darkmystic City Shrine 2

Climb in search of cinnabar gullies,
      and reach Darkmystic City.

Touching the sun: crimson clouds
      cast light on this hideaway.

If you face all that surrounds you,
      and look to the foot of the cliffs,

It's like seeing court painters' offerings—
      seeing just what they lack.

              (by the Exemplary Consort)

Written at Goldflower-Palace Taoist Refuge

Again we reach
    Goldflower's peak.

At Darkmystic City
    we sought the Way, returned.

Clouds part:
    the shape of things shows clear.

Blackness locks in:
    towers, spires, come forth.

Rain washes and the hills
    around shine clean.

Winds blow and the road
    back home moves into view.

Hills like a green-flashed screen of feathers
    channel surging streams.

What need to long for
    Penglai, that far-off faerie isle?

                  (by the Praiseworthy Consort)

Written at Goldflower-Palace Taoist Refuge 2

Bluish mists and red-struck clouds
    shimmer on our clothes.

Nighttime fog and dark green moss:
    perilous, these stone paths.

Deft, this wind, how it breathes out
    pine-tree melodies,

And the butterflies, charming—color on color
    rubbed against the face.

Together we seek those distant realms
    and, hand in hand, think long,

Pointing off toward outlying hills,
    models for eyebrows' arch.

We wish to gather body and mind
    and heart and this clear, pure place.

Tao-capped and sunset cloaked, we'd serve
    the unseen, unheard, unnamed.

(by the Exemplary Consort)

At Ultimate Virtue Buddhist Temple on Cinnabar Scenes Mountain

All around us, a river of cloud,
    at free-roaming Cinnabar Scenes,

And thanks to it, my sister and I
    gaze out at the highest zones.

Clear weather: this morning's sun comes up
    a radiant dazzle, gold.

Springs pour down, winter-chill, at night—
    like tinkling jade, they ring.

Among the pine twigs, moon arcs up;
    in shadows, a zither lingers.

Down maple paths, the winds draw scents
    from musk deer, foraging.

Offerings made in reverence:
    thin robes suit our prayers.

We ask but this, may blessings guard us,
    and grant us ease, and peace.

(by the Praiseworthy Consort)

Written at Ultimate Virtue Buddhist Temple on Cinnabar Scenes Mountain

At the mountaintop on Cinnabar Scenes
    we lodge in Buddhist halls:

Moon's jade-white wheel, sun's great gold cart,
    dwell in empty air.

A monk's canteen, quite dry, pours out
    cold emerald green.

Orchids, as if they were in bloom,
    send forth evening's red.

The warrior lords have formed their ranks
    beneath the bluish peaks;

We sheltered consorts all find places
    on these sermon mats.

The monarchs of our family line
    carry on with royal tasks,

And merit accrues throughout this age,
    throughout this far-flung land.

(by the Exemplary Consort)

Written at Skyturn Courier Station

We've roamed all round this sacred realm,
    set loose our secret moods.

A thousand miles of rivers and hills!
    For a while, we could sojourn there.

What I miss: the landscape, the winds and light—
    we haven't seen enough.

But we drive back in gold and green
    to Chengdu's crooked walls.

(by the Praiseworthy Consort)

Written at Skyturn Courier Station 2

At a verdant post house, this red pavilion
      near a capital like heaven's:

To a dreaming soul it's as if we're in
      the Greenwall Mountains still.

Just now, we've gone out to look
      at views of rivers and hills—

Yet somehow it's those rivers, those hills,
      that see *us* on our way.

(by the Exemplary Consort)

Li Xunxian (d. 926?)

Accompanying His Majesty to the Greenwall Mountains, East of the Himalayas

Following eight kingly
steeds, we've
               climbed this
holy hill.

In a
      flash, cut
off from mundane
dust—all
               phenomena
at ease.

I only fear we'll
head on
               west, join
the Great
               Queen's endless
feast—

and I worry: then
how hard
               to make
a return to the
mortal
      world.

In a Palace in Shu, Written at His Majesty's Command

Sodden trees,
            forbidden
flowers in
hidden courtyards bloom.

A drinking party
half finished,
            done:
half
    sober and half
drunk.

A misty drizzle
on rain-soaked plants—
fine jade
        steps
stretch wet.

A bell. She
        wakes,
sings
    sorrow's songs,
leans alone
on a sheltering screen.

Going Fishing, Getting Nothing

At pond's edge,
                    try
to catch brocaded
fish scales
            till day's done.

Wrapped in lotus
scent,
        in musky
caltrops,
            fall
in a secret swoon.

Here's what it's like:
to seek and
                seek
and seek for that
fragrant
            bait

and yet to know
no fish
        will mouth
your
        golden hook.

Lady Pistilstamens (tenth century)

Palace Lyrics

#3

The Dragon's Pools: nine serpentine curves
      range wide and flow on through.
With silky lines, willows snag
      the winds along paired banks.
Untouched by time, these scenes that seem
      to be the sweet moist South,
Where brilliant skiffs slip here, slip there,
      on ripples of deepest green.

#8

Spring's first day! An offering:
      these inner garden flowers,
each blossom's tender pollen parts
      a fragile dawn-cloud pink.
Kneel with them on jade-white steps
      studded still with dew—
at once, His Majesty orders, *Give them*
      to that pretty harem girl.

#10

In country palaces and villas
        strung round the capital,
softly striking gold-toned chimes
        attuned to heaven-pipes,
night after night, as moonlight brightens
        the roots of trees in bloom,
along the lakeshore, endlessly,
        we sing close harmonies.

#17

Spring's stirring winds across her face:
        her morning makeup's done.
Sly, she breaks off a blooming branch,
        walks toward the riverside.
But a spying guardian eunuch
        spots her from afar,
so she throws at a tawny warbler red
        seeds from a lovelonging-tree.

#21

Outside the palace, harem girls,
        so slim around the waist:
when one begins her riding lessons
        she's nervous, and lovely, and shy.
But once astride and on her way,
        ah, *then* she wants to go—
over and over, she drops the reins,
        and clasps that pommel, and rides!

#31

The maids compete; they brandish
        their jade-white pellet bows.
A ball flies, and it finds its mark
        within a ruffled flower.
At that, surprised and fluttery,
        songbirds scatter, rise,
and tread on lingering fallen petals
        that color the ground blush-red.

#55

Deep in the palace, a young girls' game
        next to a jade-white fence:
Spring rushes look like . . . arrows! and
        The duckweed looks like . . . coins.
But don't you know that in this nook
        of fenced-in peonies,
last night someone lost her . . . hairpin,
        all feathery filigree?

#62

The smell of orchid incense, thinning;
        the candle's light burnt down:
finished perfuming the royal robes,
        and the nightwatch done—again.
Worn out, and back in her own bed,
        she sleeps within dark red drapes,
her pillow swept by fall's west wind,
        her dreams, by winter's cold.

#86

Her gown, silk gauze so thin it shows
        the skin and flesh beneath,
in empty wooden passageways
        when summer days grow long,
she leans on the railing quite alone
        without one thing to do—
except, where the river wind blows cool,
        to read things made of words.

#142

They woke up early, those palace ladies,
        called morning greetings, smiled.
But they don't recognize the man
        who's sweeping the courtyard clean.
So, courteously, they give him coins,
        and all crowd round to ask:
Life out there, is it still like
        our lives in here—or not?

II
WOMEN OF THE HOUSEHOLD

Ms. Sun (dates unknown)

Hearing Music from a Zither

Jade-white fingers,
               red silk
strings:
         muddled, and
then pure.
            The Riverside Widows'
sorrow, their
            grief—
hardest of all to hear.
                 At first,
it's a howl,
          it's a chill wind's rush,
or soon,
        sparse rustles
like rainfall at dusk.
              When close,
a gushing
         spring breaks out
from sheer
         green stone.
Far off? Great cranes,
dark
     as time, alight
from heaven's blue depths.
Come
      the small hours,
when the melody
          stops,
you'll
       live with it,

sad and alone.
                    Night's
damp will soak
the white
                orchis clumps
in a courtyard flooded
                            with moon.

Zhang Wenji (dates unknown)

Clouds at the Creek's Mouth

A mountain creek, the mouth
   of its cleft: dense clouds
      spread wide and melt.
In mid-creek,   coming
   together at last,   they spill.
If they don't   turn back again
   to the creek
      cleft's   mouth,
then once more   in mid-creek, there,
   they will make   rain.

Bamboo at Pond's Edge

They lean close to this   pond,
   these   *Noble Ones.*
Great stems   dip
   till they
      and water   touch.
Their green—surrounded
      by waves of   other greens—
ripples,   shifts,
   day after
      day, yet   doesn't fade.

Egrets on the Shore

A sandy   shoal,
    a riverful of birds:
drumming   wings put forth
    pure   tones.
They only wait
    for higher   winds to rise—
it's not   that they have
    no heart
        for heaven's   stream of stars.

A Pair of Autumn-Blooming Mallows

Green shadows   vie,
    unstinting,   lush.
Red beauties shine
    toward   one another,
        shine and   blaze.
They don't take after
    flowers of   peach and plum
that blow careless
    in spring's   wind
        and   tumble down.

Liu Yao (dates unknown)

After an Old Song

phoenix tree in the courtyard
moon rounding on toward full

watery light in this private room
an autumn night near done

shears from the south cut it to shreds,
my loom's brocade

bits of festive dogwood fall
to the bed where I lie alone

a lovely window—but quiet, too quiet
when I turn my back to the lamp

and in darkness count the cold clock's strikes
and still can't manage sleep

In Darkness, Separation

scholar-tree flowers gone to seed
shriveled empress-leaves

flying alone, my handsome bird
calls out in the heavenly blue

his green-glinting carriage drives over clouds
lightly, far out of reach

rouge: tears spill
their tracks run red

jewel-grass aroma, come to an end
this heart too hot, too bright

that jade-trimmed belt? no sound of it
the bedroom's paintings, chilled

my zither string snaps
in the dark: nobody there

the wind moves a branch in unseasonable bloom
its shadow the moonlight's work

messenger birds, pulses a-race
fly to the west—they're gone

the ocean broad, this sky so high
and I don't know where . . .

Liu Shurou (dates unknown)

Mooring at Wuchang on Mid-Autumn Festival Night

On opposite banks,   twin cities, unyielding as hills,
And a single river   that flows on to the east.

Tonight, the full   pale Lady in the sky—
How many years ago,   old Yellow Crane Tower?

Dim and boundless,   an evening of blossoming boats;
Like mist in the distance,   the reed flowers, now it's fall.

What can anyone do?   A subtle twist in the chest.
The mountains. The passage.   And everywhere, discontent.

Huang Chongjia (dates unknown)

On Declining to Marry a Prime Minister's Daughter

Lads and lasses go out together,
gather spring's green by the lush river's edge.
I said farewell to that.
Ever since, I've stuck
to my rough-thatched shack,
making no more
than poems.

When I first dressed as a gentleman scholar,
and won a government job,
I gave up for good on girly mirrors,
on prettified eyes.

Above the crowd, straight up, restrained:
I'm an evergreen pine.
Bold aspirations held firm,
my conduct is clean:
a badge of nobility, pure white jade.

Sir, if you'd have me marry,
and serve as your son-in-law,
beg heaven for a swift trans-
formation. I'll
do it, perform it, be
it: a man.

Wang Yunxiu (724?–777)

Joining My Husband on the Long Road to the Capital

Sweep the road clean!
We'll see no trace of hunger or of cold.

Heaven shows compassion—
if your will is strong.

Stop it now, this
tearfall at farewell

and take my hand: we'll get there,
to all that waits out west.

On My Husband's Elevation to Grand Councilor: Sent to My Scornful Sisters

His Excellency is noble enough
for the ancient Hall of Fame.

And weren't *we* born to the proud clan
of the statesman, the poet Wang Wei?

When we'd just grown up—oh, then
you laughed at this pauper's bride.

Now, blush to see Lord Rags-to-Riches
as honor and wealth arrive.

Advising My Husband to Broaden His Political Base

Flutes from the south, songs from the north,
make painted rafters ring

and as dawn nears, your entertainers
slip on fresh dancers' robes.

But that prince of old threw wide his doors,
asked the best and brightest in.

He knew that rootless glory
passes, too soon, on.

Madame Zhang (mid-eighth century)

As in Olden Times

First light, and the pulley draws up
the bucket rope's undyed strands.
> Nightly, notes
> from the well-side tree
> fall on bricks' dark moss.
Trickles, rivulets, blown about, slide
like rain when the season's right.
> Washed till they gleam,
> some fine leafy greens—
> that's no use of what heaven sends!
The man I married, he doesn't get
what this is all about.
> Like the rube who watered
> his fields with a jar:
> he admires his self-
> > > > esteem.

Willow Floss

Thick with mists,
this sweet
new day in spring.
      Snowy catkins
      lift
      on greening withes.
Sometimes their flying threads
meet flowers, and both
are stirred—
      not by wind:
      they drift loose
      on their own.
Passing goblets,
they float in clear
chartreuse, and brushing
      bed drapes, stitch
      designs on
      red raw silk.
What use
restraining sadness,
making merry?
      What heart holds
      in spring can't finish
      itself off
            alone.

Bowing to the New Moon

Hail the new moon!
  Hail the moon outdoors, in front of the hall.
  Ghostly potential is caging the Tree-in-the-Moon;
  it's an empty bow not yet bent and strung.

Hail the new moon!
  Hail the moon upstairs, in the dressing room.
  A lonely mirror will settle on its stand;
  eyebrow crescents already draw in close.

Hail the new moon!
  Hail the moon—but that won't lift this mood.
  A garden of flowers rinsed clear as wind and dew:
  the moon looks down toward people bound to age,
  and people gaze off to a moon forever bright.

  The granny next door, she too hails the moon.
  Each prayer sadder, sadder—until the sound stops short.
  Years ago, she hailed the moon with a shining face,
  but now as she hails the moon, two lines of tears trail down.
  She turns, looks back at a crowd of women all hailing
                          the new moon,
  and remembers, *Once, when I was young and lived in deep
                          red rooms . . .*

Ms. Zhao *aka* The Wife of Du Gao (fl. 789)

My Husband Fails His Exams Again

It's clear as daylight: you, my dear,
possess talents extraordinaire.
How is it then, that year
after year, you get sent back to me?
So far, my lord, I've been just a wife,
too shy to face your face.

But if, my lord, you come here now,
best show up after dark.

On Hearing That My Husband Has Passed His Exams

It isn't very far from here, the capital, Chang'an:
lush with luxuriance
its prospects, its lovely
airs afloat.
You, dear, now you've got it
all—and still so young!

Tonight when you drift off
drunk, besotted, in
whose house will you sleep?

Xue Yun (fl. c. 800?)

For Young Miss Zheng

Ablaze with a bloom   like the bright Maytime,
like the Lady   of the river Luo,
behind pearl-sewn blinds,   in ornate rooms
of a winehouse, she passes   her spring.

Twenty-five   string zither, deftly
stroked: slender   fingers tease,
softly killing   them with heartache, those
boys outside   her gate.

A smile. Her whole face   opens,
powdered   to a blush, and
in the east garden,   on all those trees,
peach blossoms   give up the ghost.

> Melodies   in the morning . . .
> Melodies   in the dusk . . .

Alone, she sits before   the window:
sleek   and single, a jade-white stone.

> Winsome   when she moves . . .
> Winsome   sitting still . . .

At the sight of her,   the soul's ten parts
scatter   and melt away.

Brocaded   mats in front of the hall,
a brazier   darkly red.
In fragrant goblets suffused with   green,
she pours out   herbal wine.

She unties her sash and time   after time,
they stop: the songs, the pipes.
Within bed drapes of   hisface flowers,
musk and orchid-smell   spill.

When evening starts,   the aroma
from gauzy   clothes persists,
yet every time the candles   are doused
someone hates it: *fall's nights . . .   so short.*

Pei Shu (fl. 816–832)

Answering My Husband, Yuan Zhen

When word arrives—promoted!—
at this grand gate of ours,
willows in palace gardens
spring new
as this thought: *Stay here.*

I am not sad
you've received a post so high.
I only grieve
at leaving
all those we hold near.

It's like the old poem:
A golden finch
goes off to a venerable tree.
And so my pearly shoes will follow
the pure dust in your wake.

Yet I think: *When we finally get there,*
beyond a thousand hills,
by that sea-gray river
already
it'll be the end of spring.

Xue Yuan (late Tang?)

Self-Portrait, Sent to My Husband

Soon I'll start in with my paintbrush,
its vermilions, its azurite greens—
but first, I pick up
my precious mirror: winter-cold.

Already surprised by the worn
look of my face,
I now come to see
how the hair around it   fades.

Teary eyes are easy
enough to sketch.
This sadness in my belly?
Hard to write   *that* out.

I'm afraid that you've forgotten
everything.
Sometime, unroll this
painting.   Take a look.

Pei Yuxian (late Tang?)

Missing Him: Two Poems

1

Winds lift and curl the level
sands. Sun slips
into their dusk. Signal
smoke. A distant guess—
nomads' flocks on the move.
Called up, captured, gone sick
in the camps: some
heroes never come home.
I'll wear out my gaze on
barbarous skies. I'll
cry over clouds
on the northern front.

2

Once, love, you patrolled
the western tribes. Deployed,
you took war's force
to be no heavy thing.
Now you're gone.

You're one of the dead.

What point, this leaving
a woman like me, here
to hate the dull
half-light of another day's end?

Ms. Jiang (tenth century)

In Answer to My Sisters, Who Want Me to Stop Drinking

My whole   life, I've
          been crazy
                          for it,
wine.
          And you
knock
          yourselves   out,
pressing me
          to eat!
Just let   me have
          my cup
                          brimful:
well, then—no
          problem—I
get   through them,
          the seasons
flashing   by.

III
Courtesans and Entertainers

The Lotus Courtesan (dates unknown)

Offered to the Recluse Chen Tao

Yes, people call me
      Lotus.
My cheeks are smooth
      as jade.
That fine
      cabinet minister,
he sent this poor girl
      your way.

Hermit, if you
      won't have me,
won't do that dream-
      goddess thing,
what good's my trouble?
      Why go down?
Why try to make love
      songs sing?

Chang Hao (dates unknown)

For Madame Lu

This beauty regrets
her face, its
blushing charm,
afraid it will,
as flowers' scents fade,
end.
When the sun goes down,
she walks out
from a bright-painted hall and
stops;
below the steps she bows
to the new moon,
saluting that moon
as if she had
words she has to say,
yet those around her . . .
how *can* they
know?
Back inside,
she flings herself down
on a pillow white as jade.
Now she begins
to feel
the trace of tears let
fall.

Poem Sent Far Away

1

Year after
year, when early
March arrives,
for ten years, that's been
the time when we meet
and part.

Spring's stirring
winds know nothing
of faithfulness. Your
carriage canopy
makes its
lone slow way.

2

Today, for no
good reason, I
raise pearl-sewn window blinds,
and see the garden
flowers' first petals
fall again.

Once a human heart
takes leave, it won't
return. Yet
months and harvests
never fail. They arrive
when their season comes.

3

Pitiable and shining
lovely, a mirror
stand of jade:
dust flies, and when
will that dull veil
be brushed aside?

So: think how any pretty face
diminishes with time,
while painted eyebrows
wait—as if all's
natural—for
one good man to appear.

Shi Feng (dates unknown)

Scent-of-Delirium Cave

At the grotto's mouth,   Flying Rose-jewel
hangs plumes and   rainbows below her waist.
      Perfumed breezes   blow and flick, and lead
      a man   astray.
            Ever since by chance,   within bed drapes
            of hisface flowers, we   met,
                  who can count   the peachblow flowing
                  within that   streaming cleft?

The Pillow of the Divine Cock

A pillow painted with   love-ducks:
long in this storied   house.
      Gauze like fog,   newly sewn—
      and tussles   with a wondrous cock.
            Without my man and   drunk on dreams,
            stirred up, I   forget about dawn;
                  the cock, as well, is   loathe
                  to leave, unwilling to   cry out.

An Incense-Burner Pillow

Where has it   come from,
this odor   of secret desire?
        Musky fumes   at pillow-side—ah,
        how love   allures.
                Don't imagine   that kohl and powder
                hide   a dagger blade:
                        a jade-white beauty   offers sandalwood
                        as she   waits upon her Lord.

Soup for a Closed Door

At least I'll give   Master Playboy
a nice big   bowl,
        and when he   leaves, I'll
        call out, quick: *lock the bronze-studded door.*
                Come in through the gate   alone, he yearns
                for a passionate, talented   mate—
                        he wants to pluck   my strings, my
                        gem, play   songs of cock and hen.

A Courtesan from Xiangyang (dates unknown)

Saying Goodbye to Wu Buque

A game of Pearls Above the Shoals
    (*you've caught my drift*):
I thought my soul would melt.

Alone with this leave-taking feeling
    (*a rift in the chest*) —
I'll pour it in with the wine.

All those misty flowers out there
    (*the girls who go too far*),
they won't treat you right.

Wrong, if you make this wild sweet herb
    (*so good at heart*)
think badly of
    (*will you return?*)
her prince.

Guan Panpan (d. e. ninth century)

Swallow Tower: Three Poems

1

A guttering lamp in an upper room
      Keeps company with dawn's frost,
As one who sleeps alone arises
      From a bed that once knew joys.
How great her feeling in a single night
      Of longing, unfulfilled?
To earth's outer reaches, to horizon's end:
      Neither
           goes *that* far.

2

Cedars and pines on Graveyard Hill
      Lock in mourning's mists.
Up in Swallow Tower: thoughts,
      A quiet blaze of grief.
After they buried his sword and boots,
      Songs scattered like dust in air;
Red sleeves' perfume, a decade gone,
      Trails thin, and
           fades away.

3

Well met! Wild swans, wild geese, wheel round
      A sacred sunny slope.
And look again: how love's dark birds
      Near fall's rites, and departure.
A jade-trimmed zither, nephrite pipes,
      Senseless threads of mood—
Let them go, those spiderwebs.
      Let it go,
           that ash.

Rhyming with a Poem by Master Bo

Keeping self to my self, I guard an empty house,
      Eyebrows tight with grief—
A figure like a peony stalk
      When spring has passed away.
The gentleman can't understand
      A person's deepest thoughts—
Astonished, he speaks of an underground tomb,
      How I didn't
           go there, too.

A Courtesan from Taiyuan (d. before 828?)

Sent to Ouyang Zhan

Since we parted, I've lost my
looks, my charm:
half because I long for you, half
because of hate.
If you want to know how they look now,
those cloud-high curls—
for your handmaid's sake, see
what's inside
this casket chased with gold.

Xue Tao *aka* Xue Hongdu (c. 768–c. 832)

On the Pond, a Pair of Birds

The pair of them   light   on this deep green pond;
at daybreak, at dusk, together,   they fly out,   then home.
Thoughts fix again   on days of   raising chicks—
two hearts   one   among love's lotus leaves.

Love-Duck Herb

Green petals, green   sepals fill   fragrant steps of stone:
pair upon   pair, so small, these   ducks and drakes—
just take pleasure   in spring's long   sunny days,
pay no mind   to autumn's   early winds.

Goldenlamp Flowers

Don't you see?   By the porch rail, petals,   ruddy bronze and lush.
Below the steps, they   merely sway,   a thicket sleek and bright.
Stare close. They might   look like what thing?
A Taoist shrine in the Redwall Range   when dawn-clouds first
                                                                bank up.

Longing for Litchis

Everywhere, you hear about   that Ivory Land   in the far wild south.
The ample   flesh of its carmine   fruits—impossible   to forget.
Yet near here,   the Green Garb river   links waters with fertile Chu,
our simple juices   still a match   for those succulent   rosy jewels.

To General Gao, Who Smashed the Rebellion for the Son of Heaven

Shocked, I looked at earth and sky,   gone pale with war, and wild—
blinked, and saw   these fresh blue hills,   the old days' sunset glow.
Now I know   heaven's power   still shines,
and sun and moon,   eclipsed, can catch   its light once more.

Rhyming with a Poem Given Me by Secretary Li, at a Banquet Graced by Courtesans like Willows

A zing, and your arrow   hits its mark: in Exam Hall, top score.
Now how can we   meet again, how   expand my inch-wide heart?
Tell me, please, this splendid   scene—made beautiful for whom?
For whom these silky   yearning willows,   awash   in green-glinting
haze?

In Response to Commissioner Wu

Friar Zhi's lost flowery hermitage   could be next door to yours.
You've bought   a view of heights.   You've not crossed over yet.
In through the gate: a stream of clouds   from Bright Creek
                                                    fills the yard.
Just a step   or two   from your lofty retreat—up to empty blue.

Liu Caichun (l. eighth–e. ninth centuries)

Ah, Let Him Come Back to Me

(five lyrics from a set of six)

#1

I find no bliss
along the Qinhai's banks,
and hate with all
my life that longer
river's boats.
One bore off my
husband, carried him
away: harvest
seasons pass, and years
go by.

#3

Don't become a traveling
merchant's wife,
whose gold hairpins
pay fortunetellers' fees.
Day after day, at the river's
mouth, you'll gaze
and you'll mistake—how
many?—many
boats for his.

#4

That year, the day
he left, he
said he'd only go
a short way north.
I've seen no one
from that northern town.
But today a letter
came—from Guangzhou,
far off, in the south.

#5

Yesterday—better
than today. This
year—older
than the last.
The muddy Yellow
River may
again run clear.
Gray hairs turn to black?
Impossible.

#6

Yesterday, the northern
wind blew
cold. Boats
tied in the harbor
stayed at rest.
Waves come up and
strike; the moor-lines
snap. Shifting
oars now know
what trouble is.

Zhou Dehua (ninth century)

Willow Branches

Along one
bend of the river
Clear, a thousand
willow withes:
twenty years past,
on that old
plank bridge,
I parted from
my love.
No word
from him, no
news—this
morning still
no word.

Yan Lingbin (fl. before 881)

Nearing My End, and Inviting Guests

                    breaths?
i've still another 3, or 5
                    flowers?
2 sprigs, or 3, hang on . . .
                    to speak of parting,
just 1 cup of wine
                    we'll make our toasts
we'll never meet again

Wang Susu (fl. before 881)

Poem Using the Rhyme Words of Li Biao's Outrageous Come-on

Like, no surprise that the dawgs are out, and the chickens fly
out of control—
a skinny dude on a wasted horse, wearing
old cheap hemp.
What's-their-names must have major issues, to drag
this slacker in.
Hang on to his cash, but seriously, hustle
him on back home!

IV
WOMEN OF RELIGION

Qi Xiaoyao (dates unknown)

Song

With a laugh, I look at
          The green-dark-green sea,
So soon to turn
          To dust.

By the Royal Mother's
          Peach blooms,
I took leave of her
          Heavenly host.

A thousand years—
          Then I'll go back,
Heading off
          Beyond the sky.

With a single heart
          Will I treasure them:
These mortals, their
          Generations.

Li Ye *aka* Li Jilan (d. 784?)

On My Sickbed by the Lake, Happy Because Lu Hongjian Has Arrived

Long ago, you left: the frosts were harsh that month.
Now you've come   in a season of bitter mists.
We meet again   and still I lie here, sick,
about to speak but   first, tears fringe my eyes.
I urge on you   a recluse-poet's wine.
In return you chant   a roaming writer's poems.
I didn't think   that I'd get drunk so fast,
and yet what else   is there to do, but this?

Here by Chance

My heart's held distant:
these floating clouds,   I know they won't return,
yet heart and clouds
alike exist   where all things pass away.
Why then do these
frantic winds   trouble them, shake them so,
blowing them toward
the southern hills,   then back to the hills in the north?

Parting on a Night When the Moon Shines Clear

Two who part
without a word;   a moon without a sound:
the clear moon has
its radiant ring,   the humans, what they feel.
Once separated,
in their longing,   for lovers it's like moon's light—
up among clouds,
off on the river,   to the far peaks' highest point.

Sent to Zhu Fang

I watch the water.   I try to climb these hills.
But hills rise high   and the lake spreads out so wide.
Deep thoughts of love   know neither dawn nor dusk;
gazing far,   we pass through years, and months.
Lush hillside trees,   half-choked, grow to glory.
Meadow flowers   in endless strands unfurl.
After that parting,   feeling that knows no bounds.
When we meet again,   we'll say it all, at once.

The Tao and the Path: Thoughts Sent to Officiary Cui

Don't throw your heart away   on rootless fame.
Best think *it's not worth much—   the drive for power.*
A hundred years   the same as a day, a night,
and all you've done   disappears in what comes and goes.
Hair grayed by sorrow,   whatever you do, turns white.
A boyish face?   Not yours, for all you've learned.
No heading off   to India's holy lands;
take refuge in   your Teacher from long ago.

Zhuo Yingying (fl. e. ninth century)

Practicing My Heaven-Organ

I keep doing it: leaning   on silver-chased screens and I keep
   rehearsing on   these phoenix-pipes.
hidden hints   in the melody   make it
   rise—what I   feel   in spring.
since I keep   thinking   of what once was,
   it all   turns to useless   regret:
it's not going to   happen—I'm not   going to play
   on the goddess's   peak one note   in harmony.

Lu [*or* Hu] Meiniang *aka* Lu Xiaoyao (b. 792)

Poem Rhyming with Zhuo Yingying's "Practicing My Heaven-Organ"

—but in the women's   quarters we
   play that   mouth organ   well.
and the poet   divine   of Great White Mountain
   knows passion   from within.
someday, we'll harness   three phoenixes   white
   and drive   through vermilion   skies.
so: why grieve   for that man of   the past
   who failed to hear   your   song?

Yu Xuanji (844?–868?)

Another Poem on Riverside Willow Trees

green sparks link up
along wild riverbanks

those hazy figures move
toward distant tower rooms

shadows, reflections
stretch on waters
pure as autumn skies

and willow-pussies fall
in the hair of fishing men

roots mature
fish slip
like desires into their nooks

limbs reach low
entangling travelers' boats

a rush of rain
a night of winds and storm

the shock of dream
and then, again,
another sorrow

Depression: Two Poems

1

falling leaves whirl
and swirl, soaked through
with evening rain

alone, I strum these
red silk strings and
sing my own
clear song

if I let go
of feeling, I'll lay to rest
this grief—*lost loving*
friend, oh friend
without a heart

I'll care for my true
self, giving up
on this bitter
sea, its breakers

the clatter of rich
men's carriages: outside
my gate, they're
there

beside my pillow,
Taoists' teachings,
a stack of scrolls

done with a life
of plain cotton clothes,
I could lodge among
sky-high clouds

those verdant
waters and spring-
green hills? the time
for them is
gone

2

of course I sigh—
a passionate nature
gives enough
unhappiness

the more so when
all wind and moonlight
the garden fills up with fall

not fair: my room
like a cave yet near
the bell that tolls
the hours

night after night, a place
by the lamp and hair
that *will* turn white

Struck by a Mood at Spring's End: Sent to a Friend

orioles twitter—I startle awake
from the dregs of a dream

a touch of powder
to fix a teary face

through bamboo's darkness,
new
moon's meager light

the river's
stillness dense
with evening fog

moist mouths:
nesting
swallows carry mud

sweet fur: bees
burrow in flowers' hearts

alone, and moved to
love and pity—this brooding
knows no bounds

so I'm done with chanting
ardent lyrics, with *bent-
branched evergreens*

Written on a Wall of Abundance Temple, Built by Hermit Ren

a man who loves solitude
built this
domain of wonders

travelers find here
rest from the road

whitewashed wall
words left on it—*pointless* or
the empty

a lotus paradise
that so few know

pond dug out
springs filled it

pathways cut
the grass grew back

pagoda a hundred feet tall
gold spire like the dharma's wheel

facing the river
opens the eyes:
how it shines, that
light

Calling on the Right Reverend Taoist Mistress Zhao, Who's Not at Home

where have you
gone, with your divine
companion?

the little maid stays
in the house alone

left on the warm
hearth, a brew of herbs

in the next courtyard,
tea still steeps

a lamp flares
the murals dim

banner-pole shadows
slant long

I look with great care
look round again—

outside
these walls, so many
branches bloom

A Summer Day, a Mountain Home

this ground is where
I've come to:
a place gods might call home

thick with flowers, not
planted, not
tended, not forced

out near the garden, bent
branches for clothes-pegs

a seat by a fresh spring,
a wine cup, floating

porch rails pass into shade—
trails running deep
through bamboo

fancy silk sashes
tie up loose heaps of books

at ease I
board a bright-painted boat,
chanting *so clear, moon's light*

I trust in the breeze
it will blow, it will
carry me back

Yuan Chun (fl. before 875)

Springtime Views in the Land of Qin

Lovely, these views of spring
>from up in the Phoenix Tower:

guard posts at palace gates,
> walls within walls within walls,

and in His Majesty's garden
> trees in the falling rain—

or peaks of the seekers' range
> after the skies turn clear.

Wherever you walk, flowers
> fallen—*every*where,

and palpable, favorable airs,
> drenched, when evening comes.

Look with joy on this blessed,
> on this radiant age,

as skirts of rainbow silks
> take the path of the Taoist Way.

Hidden Meaning / Sexual Alchemy

Three thousand palace ladies
        show feathery eyebrows, arched.

Laughing, they smelt a golden ore,
        but Sun and Moon come late.

Unicorn, Phoenix, blocked by clouds—
        they mount yet they can't make it.

Forlorn and mournful, those empty hills,
        when evening's sun goes down.

Sent to My Senior Sisters in the Luoyang Region

My old home: a year
        ago, I left.

Passes and rivers: ten thousand
        miles of longing.

I write a poem to send
        on a wild goose wing,

look at the moon, think of crescent
        eyebrows, soft.

Everyone feels the sadness
        of hair gone gray.

I alone know these dreams
        of a homesick heart.

Who could bear it?—cut off
        from a land in chaos.

I hide tears, face south,
        nest on a southern branch.

Haiyin (fl. l. ninth–e. tenth century)

Nighttime, Aboard a Boat, One Text

The river's colors draw out
the colors of the sky.

These sounds of winds
whip up
the sound of waves.

A traveler
tastes bitter thoughts, of home.

Old fisherman dreams
troubles. Twitches.
Scares himself awake.

He raises oars:
cloudbanks land
before him.

Then shifts the boat.
Moon
follows in its wake.

Chant a few lines from poems.
Stop.

You still see mountains
stretched across
that horizon, far
ahead.

Notes on the Poems

Song: Wandering in Spring (p. 23): The women on view in so much earlier "palace style" poetry have shaped this imperial lady, whether we think of her as object, persona, or an autobiographical voice. (Like many poems in literary Chinese, the original can be read in either first person, or third.) Traditional metaphors evoke her beauty and sexuality. "Beneath [=inside] the grove," alludes to the Seven Sages of the Bamboo Grove, an idealized fellowship of bohemians withdrawn from politics and devoted to philosophy, wine, and poetry. The refuge this woman offers is a haven for superior souls.

An Evening Banquet as the Year Begins, Wine Cups Floating Past (p. 24): The poet celebrates a gathering sometime between the third and seventh nights of the first lunar month. Cups of liquor are being floated downstream for the revelers to snag as they pass by. The party probably took place in Luoyang, near the river from which the Empress's favored Eastern Capital took its name. Should the exhilarated courtiers emulate the charming cups and slip away, they will eventually "return"—*gui*—to more than the banquet's site. The word carries the notion of reverting to one's original unspoiled nature, to harmony with what is, the Tao.

In the Stony-Torrents Mountains (p. 25): The massif rises southeast of Luoyang. These guardian hills regulate precipitation, breaking up summer storms from the South China Sea, and in winter bringing moisture down from northerly winds. They are also charged with numinous energies. Naming the Confucian virtues of benevolence and wisdom indicates mountains and flowing waters, thanks to a line in the *Analects*: "The wise find happiness in streams, the benevolent in mountains." In two words, the poet directs our admiration to the moral qualities, to those who possess them, and to the landscape itself, which resonates with these ideals.

Plaint: Her Beautiful Letters (p. 26): An old poetic topic—women separated from their men, often by the call of duty—allows Shang-guan to explore a state of romantic obsession, perhaps with an eye to the social cost of imperial postings and war. Autumn's chilled dew coalesces; frost and old age will come. The woman's brocade screen implies an attractive boudoir. The void upon it evokes both absence of a mate and her hollow mood. In the original title, the letters she sends off are written on multicolored stationery, an indication of her fine (if futile) aesthetic sense.

from *Twenty-Five Poems upon Traveling to the Changning Princess's Floating Wine Cup Pond* (pp. 27–31): Having accompanied her husband and others to this country estate, Shangguan wrote a tour de force sequence of poems. It includes verse in the five- and seven- syllable lines predominant during Tang times, as well as difficult trisyllabics and some in four-syllable lines that carry the prestige of the classical *Book of Odes*. These last make use of such canonical ornaments as the rhyming binome *tanluan* ("brushing lushly") in #3 and the alliterative *mingmeng* ("deep and dark") in #6. Literary and historical allusions abound.

　　#6: We (or I) wish to stay, the poet says, because we've climbed to a forest like the aromatic supramundane thickets near the cool, enchanting palaces of the goddess of the moon.

　　#11: The poet takes us to a place alive with green-world energies, in a sophisticated invocation of "Encountering Sorrow," a lyric from a culture that flourished in central China in the fourth and third centuries B.C.E. These *Songs of Chu* preserve ritual quests in which a human seeker donned herbs and flowers that offered promise of contact with the divine. The "glory" that closes the poem is heiligenschein: a halolike ring of reflected and diffracted light that appears around a viewer's shadow when it is cast a long distance onto a stratum of clouds.

　　#12: The last half-line of the original reads "orchid-cassia fragrance." The phrase points to the natural excellence of disposition of highly moral Confucian role models. Pale *lan* flowers (*Arethusa japonica*, of the family *Orchidaceae*) connote inner purity, while the cassia tree (various species in genuses *Cinnamomum* and *Osmanthus*) brings to mind the heavenly Tree-in-the-Moon and valuable medicines derived from its earthbound relatives.

　　#21: The making of melodies in and about a natural landscape suggests Bo Ya, a musician of bygone times; the original nails down

the allusion, naming Zhong Ziqi, the one person who could truly understand his music. Better to *listen* to the music of nature than attempt (as poets do) its imitation.

Declining a Gift of Pearls (p. 32): A name from the long-ago Han dynasty refers to Jiang's own situation: Chen Ajiao, consort to the Martial Emperor of the Han, was neglected for a new favorite. She eventually paid the leading poet of her day (Sima Xiangru) to compose a touching *fu* named for her lonely, low-status "Palace of Gates Unending." This poem, however, undercuts the stock effect with its disdainful closure. According to the sixteenth/seventeenth-century scholar Zhong Xing, this poet's imperial husband was quite moved when his courier brought the poem from Jiang's residence—so he had the imperial Music Bureau set it to music.

For My Maidservant Zhang Yunrong, upon Seeing Her Dance (p. 33): The *Complete Tang Poems* records that Zhang was skilled at dancing to "Rainbow Skirts," the Central Asian melody associated with Yang Yuhuan herself. These images (flowerlike face pinkened with rouge and sensual energy, the sweet disorder of cloud-soft hair, a body lithe as a willow tree) would be expected here . . . or in a later poem purporting to be of mid-eighth-century origin. Similar descriptions appear in the widely known poem on Yang and her doting husband, written half a century after Yang's day by Bo Juyi.

Written on a Screen at Empty-Pond Courier Station (p. 34): This single known poem attributed to the Yifen Princess was written at a government post house on the road to the frontier. At least, so said the eunuch emissary who accompanied her out from the Tang capital, and brought the poem back. It draws together two popular poetic subjects: the emotional desolation of life in the arid north, and the fading of beauty in a woman so depressed she doesn't attend to her looks.

Teasing Lu Chang, a Bridesmaid from Down South (p. 35): When a woman known as the Yun'an Princess married, Lu Chang served as an attendant. The mythical *feng* birds (sometimes compared to the Western phoenix) and their *wutong* tree mark it as a nuptial poem.

The messenger to the gate guards for the palace women's quarters, Dong Shuangcheng (a musician-attendant of the goddess Xiwangmu), appears in other poems concerned with marriages. The color turquoise and the soaring twelve-story tower conjure up that deity's paradise. Lu is said to have cleverly responded to this poem by writing more than ten that rhymed with it.

Poem Rhyming with One by His Majesty, Written as Ordered at a Banquet in Linde Palace with a Hundred Colleagues (p. 36): Beneath a surface of praise, this exhortation carries messages about the way things ought to be. The courtiers' hands, tucked into their sleeves as they bow, imply mutual respect among what in fact were rival factions. That greatest good of Taoist philosophy, *wuwei* (nonaction), is proclaimed as the source of a well-ordered state. In Confucian political theory, the idealized ruler draws on the wisdom of those upright men who prefer a hermit's life to service under an unworthy monarch; he maintains social order by attention to decorum, even in music. The imperial grace that nurtures the people is grounded in the personal virtue of the emperor.

Poem Rhyming with One by His Majesty, Written at a Banquet in Linde Palace with a Hundred Officials (p. 37): In this poem, flattery seems to play a large role. Nonetheless, when the emperor is described as listening to advice, the moral message is clear. Praise for the beauty of the banquet scene, with its *musiciennes* warbling, leads to a comparison with Feng and Hao, capital cities of the revered semilegendary Zhou dynasty. This is something to live up to.

From *The Greenwall Pilgrimage Sequence* (p. 38–45): In 925, the two Xu sisters accompanied their royal son and nephew Wang Yan to the Greenwall Mountains, about ten miles west of Chengdu, emulating ritual mountain-tours performed by great emperors of the past. A poem by each sister was carved on memorial stones at eight locations.

Darkmystic City Shrine: The most famous Darkmystic City Shrine was located in the Tang empire's capital; that this Taoist retreat near the lesser capital of Shu had the same name must have pleased its rulers, who used Tang place names to legitimize their latter-day kingdom. Vivid descriptions of mountain scenery create a sense of transformed, and transforming, spiritual vision. Bridges (arched like dragons' backs) and high-country trails (tenuous as the flight paths of birds) add to the tricky going—in a domain of mystical change.

Darkmystic City Shrine 2: The pilgrimage has granted the poet a knowledge greater than the secondhand sort derived from paintings viewed within the confines of the court.

Written at Goldflower-Palace Taoist Refuge: The "palace" is a sanctuary on Goldflower Mountain. The landscape includes a ridge named after stylish screens trimmed with sparkling green-blue kingfisher feathers. Like others in the sequence, this poem locates itself on the homeward trip. The speaker's new perspective gives her the authority to dismiss even the fabled island paradise Penglai, home of the immortals in the pacific Eastern Sea.

Written at Goldflower-Palace Taoist Refuge 2: Here, natural features are transformed into artful sources of beauty. The curved crests of hills are said (in the nicely ambiguous original) either to be a model for women making up their eyebrows or to imitate such womanly comeliness. The sisters wish to wear headdresses marking them as dedicated to religious life, as well as capes the color of—or perhaps made from—the rose-colored clouds of sunset and sunrise that appear so often in Taoist imagery; such loveliness is reminiscent of divine "jade women." The final phrase was used by Laozi to describe the Tao itself as beyond all sight or hearing, all color and sound.

At Ultimate Virtue Buddhist Temple on Cinnabar Scenes Mountain: The beauty here is less airily transcendent than that of the "upper quarters" or "highest zones" envisioned by Taoism; it abides in the presence of pines and maples, the tranquility of moonlight and shadows and deer. The light robes donned or donated by the pilgrims have a specifically Buddhist name.

Written at Ultimate Virtue Buddhist Temple on Cinnabar Scenes Mountain: This temple's setting hints at the illusory nature of sense-impressions. The poet praises a devotion to duty that results in good karma everywhere "within the four seas"—that is, all China.

Written at Skyturn Courier Station: For all the splendor of the carriage in which she rides, this sister's final poem expresses regret at the return to the Shu capital. Its old nickname, "the tortoise walled-city," derives from the city's irregular walls, said to have been securely built (thanks to a divine message) along a tortoise's zigzag path.

Written at Skyturn Courier Station 2: Chengdu is given the flattering name "jade capital"—used in Taoist texts for the dwelling place of the heavenly emperor—but the second sister's reluctance to go home is also clear.

Accompanying His Majesty to the Greenwall Mountains, East of the Himalayas (p. 46): The Greenwall Mountains are a good bit east of the Himalayas proper, but I've added to the title to underline the original's tone. The poet evokes the mythical Kunlun range (dwelling place of the queenly goddess Xiwangmu, associated with immortality) believed to rise in the heights of the Tibetan plateau. The eight horses allude to supernatural mounts belonging to a king of antiquity.

In a Palace in Shu, Written at His Majesty's Command (p. 47): The stairway made of white semiprecious stone echoes earlier poems about lonely harem ladies.

Going Fishing, Getting Nothing (p. 48): In amatory verse from the pre-Tang period, *yu* (fish) punned on *yu* (desire). Such poems imbued garden ponds, their many-petaled flowers, and fishing itself with erotic overtones. The "golden [or metal] hook" that the elusive fish refuses suggests old slang terms for genitalia.

Palace Lyrics (pp. 49–52), *#3*: The artificial pond winds through the royal gardens, summoning nostalgia for the centuries before the Tang, when Chinese culture thrived in the alluvial Southeast.

#10: For the ethereal heaven-pipes, see the poem by Zhuo Yingying (p. 101).

#17: This palace lady could be off to an assignation. But she's caught and vents her frustration by pelting a bird, *Oriolus indicus*, with the springtime fruit of a tree, *Abrus precatorius*, whose common name translates as "thoughts of one another."

#21: If you suspect a double-meaning here, you are not alone.

#31: In an archery competition among the serving girls, a metal ball shot from a special bow hits home amid a flurry of petals gone out of control; the action climaxes as birds knock down the last of the tree-blossoms. "Tread" in the sense of "step upon" is a literal translation; it may be that all the excited birds do is hop around.

#55: This game of making up similes was later played in the garden of the great eighteenth-century novel *Hongloumeng* (*The Story of the Stone*). The discovery of an alluring hair ornament tumbled down among the sensuous flowers hints at other amusements.

#62: This aging palace lady spends her nights at the slow task of scenting her lord's robes in the smoke from an incense burner.

Hearing Music from a Zither (p. 55): This poem explores sounds and feelings emanating from the silk strings of a *chyn*. The Xiang River Consorts, sisters married to the semilegendary Emperor Xun, became an emblem of deep, tearful mourning. The language describing long-lived cranes and the vastness beyond the sky has rich associations of mysterious power.

Clouds at the Creek's Mouth (p. 57): The old euphemism for sexual intercourse, "clouds and rain," is here made new as the poem progresses from oozing mists to falling drops. The word rendered "spill" is used not only for bodily outpourings but also for a rush of emotions or words.

Bamboo at Pond's Edge (p. 57): Bamboo signals moral rectitude. It may bend when adverse conditions pile up like snow, but it does not snap. Reflected amid summer's short-lived verdure, the giant grasses maintain their distinctive hue. This allegory would apply equally well to a husband's integrity in the political realm or to a wife's fidelity to her spouse.

Egrets on the Shore (p. 58): These water birds represent unspoiled beings—the poet herself? her mate?—who harbor aspirations lofty as that celestial river, the Milky Way, but wisely await the proper time to soar.

A Pair of Autumn-Blooming Mallows (p. 58): The late-blooming shrub *Hibiscus syriacus*, or rose of Sharon, is native to parts of China. This pair seems to sustain one another, as a well-married couple does, long after passion's impetuous springtime blossoms have blown away.

After an Old Song (p. 59): The room is a nuptial chamber. The loom and the old southern state of Wu, source of fine scissors, are among the images pointing back to this poem's pre-Tang female-voice predecessors. The dogwood (which, literally, drops onto the speaker's pillow) may be worn on her head, as is customary for the ninth day of the ninth lunar month—when one would wish to be with one's nearest and dearest. The "bits" are in the original "flowers"; the flowers of genus *Cornus* are not the white petallike bracts, but the small centers that swell into berries.

In Darkness, Separation (p. 60): The poplars and paulownia trees are diminished by autumn. The "bird of Viet" in the original (perhaps a peacock or a Chinese partridge with a haunting cry) suggests that the speaker's beloved roams in the wild south. Distance has cut off the fragrance of an extraordinary "precious-jade herb"—her man. The sexy tinkling of belt-ornaments, the music of restlessness: Both are silenced, and even those other birds, the blue-green couriers between lovers, depart.

Mooring at Wuchang on Mid-Autumn Festival Night (p. 61): It is the night of the full moon in the eighth month, a time for gathering with friends and family (maybe on a pleasure boat with decorated "orchid oars")—unless one is traveling. The speaker is passing through Wuchang and its neighbor cities on the great Chang Jiang (Yangzi River). On a hill overlooking the river, a tower first built in 223 C.E. stands, reminder of immortals who took flight there, as she may not; overhead, the home of the lunar goddess shines.

On Declining to Marry a Prime Minister's Daughter (p. 62): See Huang Chongjia's bio note. The speaker shows erudition: To "gather spring's green" summons up a whole history of poems about amorous outings, just as the humble home gestures toward an impressive genealogy of high-minded recluses.

Joining My Husband on the Long Road to the Capital (p. 63): As elsewhere, I've taken the traditional Chinese editor's liberty with the title, here adding to the original's "Together with [My/Her] Husband, Traveling to Qin."

On My Husband's Elevation to Grand Councilor: Sent to My Scornful Sisters (p. 63): Wang claims for her husband status equal to the worthies whose portraits hung in an emperor's "Unicorn Hall" back in the first century B.C.E.; she then reminds her sisters of their family connection to the exemplary Wang Wei (701–761). The original poem names a man of the Warring States period who also overcame poverty and frustration, Su Qin.

Advising My Husband to Broaden His Political Base (p. 64): I follow a textual variant, "the fifth watch [3–5 A.M.]"; the alternative, "spring orchises," emphasizes the youthful, and ephemeral, sexuality of the dancers. Wang's husband did make the mistake of limiting his social (and hence political) contacts to his own clique. This poem invokes as role model a Han dynasty Grand Councilor wise enough to welcome various sage advisors to his home.

As in Olden Times (p. 65): The creaking of a well's pulley rope imagined as natural silk is heard by someone kept awake all night by longing and the sound of water falling from the courtyard's paulownia tree (the wood of which was used to make that dulcimerlike instrument, the *chyn*, associated with passionate insomnia). But this restive woman's husband resembles a clumsy and unimaginative farmer whom the witty philosopher Zhuangzi described as lugging water in an urn rather than increasing the garden's fecundity with irrigation. Worse, the man smugly considers himself to be on a par with the capable and upright men of the past.

Willow Floss (p. 66): Underlying this poem of sexual longing is an old pun: the white free-flying filaments from the catkins of willow trees are named with words that sound much like "lingering thoughts" or "thoughts of [you] staying on." The green liquor Zhang mentions wouldn't be the Chartreuse made by French monks, but it was surely equally heady.

Bowing to the New Moon (p. 67): Chinese women used to pay homage to the moon on the night of its monthly rebirth. A thin arc embraces the tree Tang readers saw spreading its branches where you may see a face; earthshine fills in the disk. In stanza two, a beauty with a round, full-moonlike mirror sees the new moon as a crescent like the arched eyebrows that adorn her forehead. Yet the brows in the mirror knit together in a frown, and a mirror decorated (as the original text tells us this one is) with a *luan*-bird was a metaphor for someone who misses an absent mate.

My Husband Fails His Exams Again and *On Hearing That My Husband Has Passed His Exams* (p. 68): These lively colloquial poems show the poet caught in the double bind of her social role: Zhao must display respect while urging her husband to work harder. She is *qie*, "I, your concubine [= humble wife]"; he is *jun*, "you, my lord" twice, and the more intimate *liangren*, "you, dear," only when she's softening him up. Yet she doesn't care to have the neighbors see him slinking home again. The second poem catches the rest of her dilemma: Now that her husband has finally succeeded in Chang'an, he's bound to be caught up in the adulation and revelry that rose around the new "PhDs" in the flourishing pleasure district of that great city.

For Young Miss Zheng (p. 69): This poem draws on the imagery of "palace style" poems, which showed women enmeshed in eroticized languor. But this woman's beauty gives her a certain power. She (is it Miss Zheng, or a fictional stand-in—for her, or even for the poet herself?) is a courtesan, skilled in music and choosy about her visitors. The attractive furnishings of her apartments enhance the elegance of her person. Her well-groomed prettiness causes the peach blossoms (in one of the vernal East Gardens cited by many poets) to wither from shame at being outdone. Yet her bed curtains' pattern of *furong* blossoms puns on *fu rong*, "[my] man's face," a hint of yearning for a love absent from her life.

Answering My Husband, Yuan Zhen (p. 71): According to a Tang source, in 829, when Pei's husband received orders sending him to serve as military governor of Wuchang—only a month after his return from another distant posting—he overheard her weeping at the news and wrote her a poem. This one responds to his. The pun on *liu si* ("willow floss / thoughts of remaining") sets up a tension between early spring in the imperial palace gardens (near the couple's home at the center of the empire) and the melancholy of spring's end at his

remote new post. Lines in the ancient *Book of Songs* about an impe-
rial-yellow bird (*ying*, an oriole or finch) removing itself to a lofty tree
indicated success in a government career. Pei praises her husband
by citing the "pure dust" said to have risen behind the chariot of the
admirable Han dynasty poet Sima Xiangru. She's also announcing
her determination to go with him.

Self-Portrait, Sent to My Husband (p. 72): The story attached to this
poem says Xue Yuan's husband, long away from home, was given in
marriage the daughter of an official who wished to keep him around.
At the prospect of losing her husband, Xue sent him a self-portrait,
along with the poem. Sitting down to paint the image on which her
future depends, the speaker feels a chill as she contemplates her
once-prized metal mirror, as cold to the touch as the winter that
ends the life of a year. The husband, we are told, was moved, and
the two were reunited.

Missing Him: Two Poems (p. 73): The hero named in the original was
Li Ling, who in 74 B.C.E. died of illness in captivity after fighting an
Inner Asian people, the Xiongnu, for the emperor.

In Answer to My Sisters, Who Want Me to Stop Drinking (p. 74): The sisters
to whom the poem is addressed could be paternal cousins. Courtesans
and women in religious life also used such familial language, but
there is no record of this poet's lifestyle taking one of those turns.

Offered to the Recluse Chen Tao (p. 77): "The Lotus Courtesan" was
dispatched to wait upon this mountain-dwelling hermit, but he re-
fused her services. Her saucy response employs language from much-
quoted Han era poems about a dream-state night of love between a
mountain goddess and a mortal king. This translation is freer than
most, to catch the doubleness of the key terms—atmospheric, but
by Tang times, frank.

For Madame Lu (p. 78): The painted hall implies the residence of a
palace lady, or (more likely) of another courtesan.

Poem Sent Far Away (p. 79): The jade stand for a makeup mirror would suggest to readers in the know a pretty image of a woman's genitalia.

Scent-of-Delirium Cave (p. 81): The story goes that Shi Feng would rate prospective clients in seven hierarchical categories, each bearing the name of one of her extant poems; most of the titles describe luxurious boudoir furnishings (e.g., "Chained-Lotus Lamp" or "A Quilt of Crimson Mermaid's-Cloth"). This first poem interweaves the mystical, the sexual, and the Taoist quest for immortality in the flesh, inscribing the courtesan's body as divinely beautiful and life-giving, capable of pleasure and of pleasuring. "Flying Rose-jewel" is a desirable handmaiden of Xiwangmu, associated with otherworldly erotic encounters. The cave mouth evokes the paradise-caverns of Taoist lore, as well as the uterine source of life. The bedding's decorative flowers bring up the old pun on "[my] man's face." Peach blossoms floating on a stream through a narrow valley—an emblem of longevity in the cave-utopia described by the pre-Tang poet Tao Qian—evoke the female genitalia some have perceived in the peach fruit of immortality and the orchard flowers belonging to Xiwangmu.

The Pillow of the Divine Cock (p. 81): The second poem in the sequence teases: the speaker, dressed in a diaphanous gown, has a pillow (probably ceramic) decorated with that symbol of amorous fidelity, the Mandarin duck and drake. She dreams of a godlike, or prodigious, chicken (apparently male, since it is expected to crow). That she struggles with him suggests the battle metaphors in Taoist descriptions of sexual intercourse as a means to longevity.

An Incense-Burner Pillow (p. 82): In the Chinese, this fifth poem of the original seven opens with "Han Shou's scent," referring to a good-looking fourth/fifth-century man and the bold young woman, Jia Wu, who arranged his secret nighttime visits to her room. She gave him some marvelous incense purloined from her father; its lingering scent revealed the affair. Perhaps the poem reassured less worldly guests: It compares the beauty performing her services—cool and perfect as polished jade—to a divine woman (a nymph or deva) who burns incense at a Buddhist altar.

Soup for a Closed Door (p. 82): The sequence's last poem reveals that would-be clients rated lowest were sent on their way after receiving only a bowl of broth in a vestibule. The object of the visitor's desire is compared to the beautiful second-century B.C.E. poet Zhuo Wenjun; the story goes that her elopement with the male poet Sima Xiangru had its start when she heard him playing a *chyn*. (The polished instrument here is said to be "gemmy" or "like fine jade"—a description that in context seems to gesture toward the courtesan's own prized body.) The poem's conclusion turns on the beautiful music the unsuccessful suitor wants to make: "Male-and-Female Phoenix," a reference to the melody Sima played that fateful night, the lyrics of which describe a male *luan*-bird searching for an elusive female, that they might fly together.

Saying Goodbye to Wu Buque (p. 83): This clever poem was written after Wu and a companion encountered the courtesan on a mountainside in what's now Hubei province; the translation's parenthetical phrases lay out implications of resonant phrases and double meanings. Just as "prince" (*wangsun*, "royal scion") carried from long-time usage the un-uttered word "return," so "sweet [literally, "fragrant"] herb" had been glossed since the antique *Songs of Chu* as a metaphor for inner virtue.

Swallow Tower: Three Poems (p. 84): See the poet's biographical note on page 140. Graveyard Hill, where nobles of the past were buried, lies north of the old capital, Luoyang. The reader's sense of Guan's grief is intensified by images of past happiness: Red sleeves appear in many pleasant poems as metonym for a beautiful woman and the migratory swallow—indicated by "love's dark birds"—a traditional love symbol. Now, as the autumn sacrifice to the earth god approaches, flocks swirl like memory, emotion, and the melodies of days gone by.

Rhyming with a Poem by Master Bo (p. 85): The resting place of the one for whom the speaker mourns is set clearly in the underworld. The perceptive reader (of poems or persons) would understand, from her tightly knit eyebrows and wasted body, Guan's feeling for the man who died. But Bo Juyi has chided her for shallow-heartedness—so she will present him with a more obvious corporeal sign, her death.

Sent to Ouyang Zhan (p. 86): Hair done up in the style called *yunji* ("cloudy topknot") is severed from the speaker's languishing body; it bespeaks that body's imminent end.

On the Pond, a Pair of Birds (p. 87): These loving waterfowl may be the Mandarin duck and drake of conjugal bliss, who mate for life. Their "two hearts one," like the lotuses that pun on "love," set this poem in the tradition of female-voice amatory verse. Who thinks so deeply, even longingly, of the breeding season to come? Perhaps the birds, perhaps the one who chants the poem. Or perhaps her audience.

Love-Duck Herb (p. 87): The "duck-and-drake plant" of Sichuan puts forth buds in facing pairs, resembling birds that fly together like faithful Mandarin ducks. Readers must decide whether the birds are being admired or criticized for their *carpe diem* attitude—and so, whether we are being admonished to follow suit, or not to.

Goldenlamp Flowers (p. 87): Riddle poems were popular in Xue's day. Chanted without a title, this one would have allowed her to entertain banquet guests. The flower has been identified as *Tulipa edulis*; a sixteenth-century Chinese botanical work describes the blossoms as ruddy and lantern-shaped. Since they've also been called "eternal-spring flowers," the closing's hint of the Taoist quest for longevity is apt. The shrine known as the Redwall Palace is a religious retreat located west of Chengdu, in the Redwall (*aka* Greenwall) Mountains.

Longing for Litchis (p. 88): The yearning for their sweet liquidity is part of litchi lore. The best litchis come from China's far south, including the Qin and Han dynasty outpost known as "ivory [or elephant] commandary." By Tang times, this red-skinned fruit was also being grown in Xue's home region, as well as in adjacent territory once part of the exoticized kingdom of Chu, along the central Chang Jiang. Since the word meaning "close to (here)" can also be taken as "recently," the poet may be alluding to the contemporary spread of litchi cultivation: "Recently, [litchi bushes leafed out as if wearing] green/blue clothes [= servants' livery] are connecting with the streams of Chu." The river Green Garb (*chingyi*) flows into the Min—a tributary of the Chang Jiang—just south of Chengdu, so its waters do indeed eventually join with Chu's.

To General Gao, Who Smashed the Rebellion for the Son of Heaven (p. 88): In 805, Xue Tao's long-time protector, Military Governor Wei Gao, died; one of his generals—supported by the Chengdu garrison—seized control. But imperial forces under Gao Chongwen retook the area. Although the rebel leader was executed, the people were not held accountable, so Xue would have been exonerated if she'd continued to serve as hostess under the breakaway regime. Nonetheless, a poem praising the new governor, Gao, was a wise move.

    Xue's words reflect the notion that social and political order correspond with the ordering of celestial phenomena. Gao is praised for rescuing the poet's world from chaos, a boon like the return of normal color and light after the unsettling dimness of an eclipse.

Rhyming with a Poem Given Me by Secretary Li, at a Banquet Graced by Courtesans like Willows (p. 88): The Chinese title does not refer explicitly to courtesans or trees, but the representation of womanly beauty by willows allows Xue to compliment the guest of honor, whose identity is uncertain. Again, the Chinese for "silk-floss willows" puns on "think of staying." The custom of presenting a broken-off withe to one departing may mean Li was leaving Chengdu.

    Xue predicts, or commemorates, Li's success in the civil service exams, which had been held, back during the Jin dynasty, in a site actually known as East Hall. Earlier, during the Han, candidates shot arrows at the bamboo slats mentioned in Xue's original text—slats on which were written various essay questions. Like poets before her, she uses the phrase "inch[-wide] heart" to stress the overwhelming extent of her feelings as she salutes Li.

In Response to Commissioner Wu (p. 89): "Friar Zhi," a learned fourth-century monk, built a temple alongside Bright Creek on sacred Mount Tiantai and spent much of his life in semiseclusion. What enters the compound around Wu's place is ambiguous: It may be mists rising off some other bright creek, or anyone who visits, or the poet herself, on a call occasioning the poem. She implies that Wu's experiences in his retreat ("lofty" both physically and spiritually) have taken him to a state just short of the incomprehensible vastness of the heavens.

Ah, Let Him Come Back to Me (pp. 90–91): Expansion of long-distance commerce during the Tang meant many women experienced extended separations from husbands on the road—or often, on the transportation network of China's waterways. These melancholy lyrics reportedly suited the lost melody to which they were sung; the title is a dialect phrase from the lower Chang Jiang region.

 #1: Winehouses lined the bank of the Qinhai where it passed through the flourishing city that is now Nanjing, before flowing into the larger Chang Jiang.

 #3: Presumably the diviner would be asked about the success of a husband's journey and the time of his return.

 #4: The northern town is Tonglu, far closer to where Liu lived than is Guangzhou.

Willow Branches (p. 92): Several rivers in China are called "Clear River"; the phrase has also been used descriptively.

Nearing My End, and Inviting Guests (p. 93): According to the memoir of Chang'an's pleasure quarters that preserved this poem, Yan took mortally ill and, as spring and her life both drew to their close, sent a boy to show the poem to young men on the way up, inviting them to a banquet. As she'd hoped, many wrote elegiac poems that did indeed live on past her death. The number missing from her text's countdown, "4," is a near-homophone in Tang Chinese for "die."

Poem Using the Rhyme Words of Li Biao's Outrageous Come-on (p. 94): As my expanded title points out, Li had annoyed the poet. Sun Qi's memoir tells us Li and a couple friends visited Wang in her elegant establishment. After considerable drinking, Li wrote on the window (not glass, but a translucent silk or pricey paper) a poem intimating he would become Wang's lover, and be granted the special favor of staying in her chambers. Wang responded, "Who's keeping this young gentleman here? Don't talk crazy talk!" Then she trumped Li by using the same three rhyme words he did, in the same order, but replacing his inflated images with chiding for déclassé rusticity. Her withering language shows the slamming effects that could be achieved by Tang poets working with noncanonical diction.

Song (p. 97): Suzanne Cahill suggests this poem may have been the vow made by a Taoist novice taking holy orders. The promise of compassion for the laity reminds us that such women pledged themselves to good works as well as practices aimed at liberation from the human condition. Xiwangmu, the "Western Motherqueen" or "Royal Mother," offered special protection to women who did not live within the walls of a family compound. The "flowers" in the original poem must be the blooms of this deity's orchard, in which the peaches of immortality grow. The color-word used for the shifting waves alludes to the eons during which dry land submerges only to rise up and then be drowned again.

On My Sickbed by the Lake, Happy Because Lu Hongjian Has Arrived (p. 98): Lu (d. 804, better known by his official name Lu Yü) was part of the same Pléiade of writers Li belonged to. He esteemed those greats of the pre-Tang era, wine-loving Tao Qian and the wild-lands poet Xie Lingyun. Li refers to these literary heroes by name in lines five and six of the original.

Here by Chance (p. 98): Li's use of a Buddhist term at the end of the first sentence, to speak of this world's ephemerality, is reminiscent of the nonsectarian thinking of her friend, the monk Jiaoran.

Parting on a Night When the Moon Shines Clear (p. 99): The last of the remote sites to which the couple's mutual longing (like the moon's light) extends is the highest peak of the Kunlun mountains; its name means "City of Multilayered Walls." All three places are impossible to stand firmly on; there is no promise of satisfaction for desire's ache.

Sent to Zhu Fang (p. 99): Zhu (fl. 786) was another member of the talented coterie of poets around the monk Jiaoran who eschewed careers in officialdom. Among his twenty-five known poems is a farewell to Li Ye that suggests a close connection.

The Tao and the Path: Thoughts Sent to Officiary Cui (p. 100): Change and old age will triumph over the most diligent and ambitious; any follower of the Buddhist path knows this. That said, Li takes a Taoist swipe at the tendency of enthusiasts to hit the road in search of spiritual wisdom. Rather than making a pilgrimage to the homeland of Buddhism, Cui ought to stay put, relying on the teachings of the Buddha, to whom she refers by a title Tang Taoists used.

Practicing My Heaven-Organ (p. 101): The *sheng* is played by blowing into a small gourd from which thirteen reed pipes rise. It resembles the mythic *feng* bird resting with wings folded upward, and its wailing music is like the cry of that high flyer. In Tang times, the ancient instrument was usually played by women; it stimulated thoughts of beings from celestial realms. The poet—stirred by the breathy music she makes as she mouths the instrument—longs for a tryst on mystical Mount Gou. This is the realm of Xiwangmu, patron goddess of romantic meetings between spiritual seekers and divinities.

Poem Rhyming with Zhuo Yingying's "Practicing My Heaven-Organ" (p. 101): This response poem dismisses Zhuo's loss of a man represented by the Taoist who achieved transcendence on Mount Gou—and played the heaven-organ with surpassing skill. The desire Zhuo experiences may yet be satisfied: if not by exercises in the women's apartments, then by an encounter with someone like the resident spirit of a mountain near the Tang capital or the great-hearted poet, Li Bo. Perhaps Lu suggests that she herself can help her friend achieve a rapturous elevation.

Another Poem on Riverside Willow Trees (p. 102): The poet knows the equation "willow = lovely woman / courtesan" too well. These trees have a sexualized existence; the word used for "hue, appearance" connotes the sensuous, reinforcing the color-word itself—the flashing green-blue of kingfisher feathers used in eye-catching hair ornaments. The erotic charge reappears in the misty line of trees, in the multistoried buildings toward which they lead the eye (conventionally, the residence of beauties who pine for mates), and in diction found in earlier amatory verse, "roots" and "fish." The latter word puns: Lurking in the wet caverns shaped by swollen rootstock, we find "desire." I've replaced the original "heads" with "hair."

Depression: Two Poems (p. 103): I've double-translated one phrase: The speaker regrets that she has no "heart-friend," and/or she regrets some friend's heartlessness. Yu draws on Buddhist language—the "bitter sea" is an apt figure for a world in which (like someone flailing about in salt water) she tearily grasps after what won't really bring happiness. She also declares her Taoist aspirations to exchange an ordinary life for the richly-robed roamings of an adept. Yet this seems a forced choice; her youthful green-time is over, so she might as well turn to the spiritual life. In the second poem, the speaker tries to retreat from the distractions of gentleman callers. (Referring to her room as a "cave" simultaneously declares that it's remote as a recluse's and, in a conventional pun made ironic by her loneliness, a nuptial chamber.) But she can't escape the sound of watchmen marking—with bell or drum—the passage of time.

Struck by a Mood at Spring's End: Sent to a Friend (p. 105): I follow Jan Walls's proposal that the Chinese phrase that I have translated as "bent-branched evergreens" looks like a song title; such trees evoked longevity and constancy. Karashima Takeshi believed this poem was written after her patron Li Yi turned Yu out, perhaps leaving her near the river named in the Chinese, the Chang Jiang. The sleeper is wakened by orioles, diurnal birds that in Chinese poetry sing like lovely women. Is it the dream that made her weep, or her return to light of day?

Written on a Wall of Abundance Temple, Built by Hermit Ren (p. 106): In writing a poem literally *on* a temple wall, Yu did what other literary visitors might, yet she points out such gestures are in the end *kong* ("in vain" and what Buddhists call "emptiness," *shunyata*). The original refers to this temple as a "lotus palace," defining the place as a Pure Land, albeit an unrecognized one. The earth welcomed the temple; the digging of a pond uncovered water as refreshing and essential as the dharma. Perhaps the pagoda—which may have borne the cosmological name Golden Wheel—was topped with a gilded finial of rings (cosmographic vestige of round Indian stupas ancestral to the squared-off Chinese towers). Certainly, it lives up to the Buddhist associations of the Sanskrit word *chakra*, "wheel," as its brightness gleams and the viewer sees anew.

Calling on the Right Reverend Taoist Mistress Zhao, Who's Not at Home (p. 107): Yu uses an intriguing poetic trope—the triggering of insight by the absence of a recluse one has come to visit. The poet takes a final look round the cloister, with its characteristic banners and wall paintings of celestial scenes, and leaves word of her visit. The last image zooms in on the flowery allurements that have drawn Zhao away. This advanced female adept may have gone a-roving with a troupe of immortal spirits. Or perhaps there's a tryst with just one.

A Summer Day, a Mountain Home (p. 108): Karashima offered evidence that this poem was written outside a city now part of Wuhan, in central China, where Yu may have sojourned. We are shown the happy beauty of withdrawal from society: Things human-made shade off into the self-sustaining natural realm. This holy zone offers a fine place for drinking; discarded clothes dominate ornamental trees and the delights of literature. The poet opts to leave on a party boat—yet she's certain the wind, in its natural way, will return her to these hills.

Springtime Views in the Land of Qin (p. 109): In praising vistas seen from within the imperial palace complex, this poem praises by implication the emperor and his reign. Yet there's subtle complaint in the emphasis on the walls surrounding the women's quarters, in the shift from the garden courtyard to the mountains south of the capital (where one might devote oneself to a spiritual lifestyle), and in hints of excess around the flowers and the auspicious—but perhaps muggy or cloying—seasonal, scented winds. Although they wear gowns suggesting romantic love, the harem women devote themselves not to the transitory pleasures of spring, but to Taoist teachings. Is this fact or wish or some of each?

Hidden Meaning / Sexual Alchemy (p. 110): Only the first half of this cryptic text is recorded in the *Compete Tang Poems*, but the whole poem appears (with the next one) in a late Tang anthology, the *Youxuanji*. It has also been attributed to another ninth-century poet, Li Tong. In the original text, the speaker observes the pretty "moth[-antenna] eyebrows" of the women attached to the emperor. They attempt Taoist alchemy, but fail: The magical one-horned beast (*lin*) and mythical bird (*feng*)—like "sun and moon"—allude to spiritually advanced saints and sages. Is the allegory here one of eros frustrated, or of a union between divine and human attempted, but denied? A distinction between sexual and sacred misses the point.

Sent to My Senior Sisters in the Luoyang Region (p. 111): Yuan's elder sisters back home may well have been her sisters-in-religion. She praises their beauty with the familiar image of eyebrows resembling the arched, feathery antennae of a moth. Migrating wild geese are a symbol of letters to faraway loved ones, often those from whom one is separated by war. The final two lines allude to one of the "Nineteen Old Poems" (perhaps dating from the second century C.E.): There, a homesick bird from the southland nests on a south-facing branch.

Nighttime, Aboard a Boat, One Text (p. 112): This poem conjures the loneliness and visionary sensitivity of a traveler taking a boat upriver toward the perilous gorges marking the entrance into the Sichuan basin. Awash with unsettling perceptions, the traveler and the old man poling the boat approach the misty narrows. Sheer peaks loom—seemingly without a gap. At this sight, the heart's-ease of poetry breaks off.

Notes on the Poets

Women of the Court

Ms. Changsun, the Wende Empress (601–636) came from an aristocratic family based in the capital of the Sui Dynasty, predecessor to the Tang. Her marriage to the charismatic Li Shimin (600?–649) strengthened a key political and military alliance. She was about seventeen when the general who was her father-in-law, aided by her ambitious young husband, was proclaimed first ruler of the Tang. Her husband took the throne in 626; he looked to his empress as a respected advisor. Changsun authored a book of moral instruction called *Precepts for Women: An Essential Record*. Her posthumous title, *Wende* (Cultured), announces her character.

Empress Wu Zhao *aka* **Wu Zetian** (c. 627–705): Born to wealth and pedigree, Wu entered the harem of the Wende Empress's husband at a young age. After his death, she attracted the eye of his son and successor; in time, she was installed as that emperor's chief wife and ruled openly beside him. In 690, after the abdication of the second of her sons to be placed on the throne, Wu became sovereign. A new dynasty with the glorious old name of Zhou was soon declared. But in 705, the aged and sickly Empress was forced to yield. Her son Li Xian (Zhongzong, ruled Jan–Feb 684 and 705–710) and the dynastic name of Tang were both restored. Of the forty-seven surviving poems under Wu's name, most are lyrics for stately court music, filled with classical references; this raises the possibility of a learned ghostwriter.

Shangguan Wan'er *aka* **Shangguan Zhaorong** (664–710) was an infant when her paternal grandfather and other men of their elite clan were executed for conspiring to dethrone Empress Wu. (See above.) Sent as a slave to the imperial palaces, Shangguan eventually won an influential position as the empress's personal assistant. She became a consort of Wu's son Li Xian; her duties were largely administrative and literary, and her title, "Zhaorong," marks a high rank. She also worked closely with Li Xian's empress, the true power holder after Wu's death. Thirty-two poems have been preserved: a small fraction of her work.

Jiang Caiping (fl. 713, d. 756?): The historical reality of this woman has been seriously questioned, but at very least she represents a recurring literary type grounded in real women's experiences. We're told a powerful eunuch selected her for the young emperor Li Longzhi (Xuanzong, r. 712–56), in part because of her poetic talent. Becoming a favorite, she was called the Plumflower Consort, a name suggesting beauty and a refined sensibility. But in time, her husband devoted himself to his Cherished Consort Yang (see below) and in 756, Jiang was left behind when the emperor fled rebel forces. Only this single poem in the *shi*-form exists, as well as one long *fu*. She is said to have composed at least seven works in that demanding form.

Yang Yuhuan, the Cherished Consort (717?–756): During her time in a Taoist convent, Yang took the religious name Taizhen. But she is best known as Yang Guifei—Yang the Cherished (or Esteemed) Consort—the title given her by the emperor of the Tang's golden decades, Li Longzhi. No other poem of hers survives; this one suits her own reputation as a skilled dancer. The facts of Yang's biography are murky, in part because she was on the losing side in factional politics. There's also a scandal being hidden. Before leaving the convent for Li Longzhi, Yang was consort to an imperial prince. The father's takeover of a woman from his own son's harem gave rise to falsifications in records of her early life. Yang's time in the convent served the same end, as well as allowing a period of purification between spouses.

The Yifen Princess (fl. 745): This intelligent and beautiful woman ran afoul of the marriage politics practiced by the Tang government: Chinese "princesses" were sent to marry non-Han leaders in bordering territories as tokens of friendship and prestige. Typically, the Yifen Princess was not the emperor's biological child, but a daughter of an important clan, elevated in rank and dispatched to a different culture, far from home—in what's now Inner Mongolia.

Song Ruoxin *aka* **Song Ruoshen** (and wrongly, Ruohua) (d. 820?) was the eldest of five sisters born into a scholarly and literary family; all five preferred study to marriage. Their one brother has been described as "uneducable." The girls' reputations for intelligence, literary skill, and classical learning reached the emperor Li Shiji (Dezong, r. 779–805). In 788, they were summoned to the capital and entered the emperor's household. Ruoxin and the three youngest sisters became imperial concubines; all five regularly exchanged poems with the emperor and the men of his court. Ruoxin was appointed Controller of the library in the palace complex in 791 and was posthumously awarded high rank. A book believed to be her *Analects for Women* (with commentaries by her sister Ruozhao) was for centuries a standard text for girls' education.

Song Ruozhao (d. 825): Ruozhao was the second-born of the five Song sisters. She took a high post in the hierarchy of the inner palaces and oversaw the education of imperial offspring, including the next three emperors. She reportedly wrote several books of poems and prose. After her elder sister's death, Ruozhao took over Ruoxin's duties in the palace; in time, she was named to a key position overseeing records and communications in the imperial women's quarters. She was posthumously enfeoffed as Lady of the state of Liang.

Song Ruoxian (d. 835): Ruoxian was the fourth-born of the remarkable Song sisters. After the death of Ruozhao, Ruoxian succeeded her sisters in office. Her abilities were regarded especially highly by the literary-minded emperor Wenzong (Li Ang, r. 827–840). But in 835, she ran afoul of factional politics raging around the throne and, at the urging of a powerful palace eunuch, she was ordered to commit suicide. In addition to the single entry for Song Ruoxian in the *Complete Tang Poems*, at least four other extant poems have been proposed as her work.

Praiseworthy Consort Xu, Obedient and Sagely Queen Mother of Shu (c. 883–926) and **Exemplary Consort Xu, Respectful and Sagely Dowager of Shu** (d. 926): These poets came from an impoverished family of Chengdu. Known for their beauty and their poetry, they were taken as consorts by Wang Jian (847–918), the bandit-turned-general who emerged as military governor, and then independent ruler, of Shu (now western Sichuan) in the war-torn years surrounding the Tang empire's collapse. Wang's capital was a haven for literati and artists in that difficult era. When his son Yan ascended to the throne, both women were promoted to ranks suiting the mothers of princes and wielded considerable power. They—and Wang Yan—were killed after Shu's conquest by a short-lived dynasty called the Later Tang.

Li Xunxian (d. 926?), daughter of a Persian immigrant, had a reputation as a poet. She became a consort of Wang Yan, dissolute monarch of the state known as [the First] Shu—which broke away from the Tang early in the tenth century, only to fall in 925. Wang Yan's consorts were killed along with him, and his father's widows (see above), the following year.

Lady Pistilstamens (tenth century): In 1958, it was argued that two poets wrote under the flowery name "Lady Pistilstamens," one of them the Exemplary Consort Xu of Shu. (See above.) But the author of these poems has traditionally been identified as a consort of Meng Chang (919–965), monarch of a successor state in the same region called the Later Shu. When the Mengs' two-generation kingdom fell to the expanding Song empire in 965, this Lady Pistilstamens (along with the royal library) was taken into the imperial palace. Perhaps each woman wrote some of the thirty-two Palace Lyrics in the two collections unearthed in the eleventh century from the disordered Shu archives. Certainly, some of the 157 Palace Lyrics now ascribed to Lady Pistilstamens are spurious; others may be later recoveries.

Women of the Household

Ms. Sun (dates unknown): This talented poet, wife of the literatus Meng Changqi, ghostwrote poems for her husband, but a tenth-century source says she burned her work on the grounds that literary brilliance is not for women. The same story is found in accounts of later female writers; it may have been a free-floating biographical factoid indicating the *type* of person someone was perceived to be. Three poems survive.

Zhang Wenji (dates unknown) was married to a military staff officer named Bao Canjun. Only these four of her poems remain.

Liu Yao (dates unknown) has three poems recorded in the "unverified women" chapter of the *Complete Tang Poems*; they also appear in an early tenth-century anthology, *Caidiao ji*.

Liu Shurou (dates unknown): One poem, and no other information, survives.

Huang Chongjia (dates unknown): The chief source of information on this poet is a late tenth-century compendium, the *Taiping guangji*, that runs heavily toward fictionalized material. It tells us Huang, accomplished daughter of an official in what is now Sichuan, was orphaned young and at age thirty had not married; she cross-dressed by adopting the blue robe of a scholar. Imprisoned in circumstances surrounding a fire, Huang sent a poetic appeal to the region's prime minister. He, impressed by the intelligence of the supposed young man, offered Huang employment and in time, his daughter in marriage—hence, the poem translated here.

Wang Yunxiu (724?–777), daughter of a military governor, was married to Yuan Zai, who rose from relative poverty to the high office of Grand Councilor after she accompanied him to the capital and helped him study for the civil service exams. When her husband was forced to suicide as the result of political intrigue, Wang was summoned to join the imperial household, probably in recognition of her literary gifts. But she resisted, choosing death.

Madame Zhang (mid-eighth century) was married to the poet and official Ji Zhongfu, celebrated as one of the "Ten Talents of the Dali Reign Period" (766-780). Five of her poems have been preserved, along with fragments of three others.

Ms. Zhao *aka* **The Wife of Du Gao** (fl. 789): A Tang source refers to this poet as Ms. Liu. Her husband did, indeed, pass the government's highest level exams in 789; he went on to a career of more than thirty years, rising to the rank of Minister of Works. The *Complete Tang Poems* records four of Zhao's poems, plus a possible fifth said to have been written on Du's behalf. A sixth is attributed to her in a sixteenth/seventeenth-century anthology, *Mingyuan shigui*.

Xue Yun (fl. c. 800?): Three of her poems still exist. One Tang anthology, the *Youxuanji*, records her family name as "Jiang," and there are two different writings of her given name; this suggests her work had considerable informal circulation, copied out by one reader for the next.

Pei Shu (fl. 816–832) was wife to one of the leading poets of the mid-Tang, Yuan Zhen (779–831). In 816 she became successor to the woman for whom he wrote several famous elegies.

Xue Yuan (late Tang?): Xue Yuan may have lived during or after the fall of the Tang. Her husband's name was Nan Chucai and she reportedly excelled as both a writer and a painter.

Pei Yuxian (late Tang?): Contemporary researchers disagree on whether "Pei" is this poet's surname, or her husband's. Her two known poems were recorded in the "unverified women" chapter of the *Complete Tang Poems*; they also appear in the early tenth-century *Caidiao ji*.

Ms. Jiang (tenth century) lived in the prosperous independent state called Wu Yue, longest-lasting of the kingdoms that arose as the Tang empire broke up. She was a daughter of Jiang Ning, who served on the staff of a Tang prince and produced a collection of long *fu* poems. Her husband Lu Meng was a Wu Yue administrator in what's now Zhejiang province.

Courtesans and Entertainers

The Lotus Courtesan (dates unknown) is said to have come from modern Jiangxi province.

Chang Hao (dates unknown): In addition to the two poems translated here, a sixteenth/seventeenth-century anthology, *Mingyuan shigui,* attributes two more to this courtesan.

Shi Feng (dates unknown): According to the *Yunxian zaji* (Miscellaneous Records of Cloudy Immortals, compiled by a twelfth-century man from what is now Anhui province), Shi was a courtesan who'd lived in the same area. It seems she had both wit and a flair for marketing.

A Courtesan from Xiangyang (dates unknown): Only this poem and the anecdote attached to it have been preserved.

Guan Panpan (d. e. ninth century): The story goes that Guan, a well-known courtesan of Xuzhou (in what's now Jiangsu province), became concubine of an official named Zhang Jianfeng. He built "Swallow Tower" for her, and after he died she remained there alone for more than a decade. When the famous Bo Juyi (772–846) wrote poetry criticizing her for not suiciding (in accordance with Confucian notions of "chastity" for widows), Guan responded in tears, saying she lived only to protect Zhang's reputation, lest so drastic an action by a concubine give him notoriety in the realm of sexual matters—whereupon she wrote poems using Bo's rhyme words, stopped eating, and died about ten days later. Some twentieth-century scholars have questioned this version of the sequence in which the various poems were written.

A Courtesan from Taiyuan (d. before 828?): All that is known about this woman is the story surrounding the poem translated here. When the scholar-official Ouyang Zhan (785?–827?) visited Taiyuan, the two formed a relationship; upon his departure, Ouyang promised to send for her. He did not, and, we are told, she cut off her hair, wrote the poem for him, and died.

Xue Tao *aka* **Xue Hongdu** (c. 768–c. 832) lived in Chengdu; her family originated in Chang'an. Her father, a government functionary, died when she was young. She became a courtesan and protégée of a powerful military governor, hostessing at official gatherings. Word of her cleverness and talent spread; literary men exchanged verses with her—doing so was evidently something of a coup. Xue eventually adopted the garb of a Taoist adept, living outside the city, near where the great poet Du Fu had also taken on the role of semi-recluse. Her penchant for invigorating, sometimes racy colloquialisms does not fit the norms of elite verse; that is not what she needed to write and often her diction suggests impromptu composition at a party. Other poems show she had the capacity to pick up on the bits of canonical learning she could glean from her place in life. They can be found in *Brocade River Poems.*

Liu Caichun (late eighth–early ninth centuries) lived in the lower Chang Jiang region. Her husband, Zhou Jicong, was also a performer. Liu's repertoire ran to 120 songs, and she was known for her moving renditions of the popular melody to which the lyrics translated here were set. Liu is cast in one account as a rival of Xue Tao (above) for the attentions of the eminent poet Yuan Zhen. A late Tang collection of romantic tales tells us that when Yuan was posted to Liu's area, he became so infatuated with her that he lost interest in a previous relationship with Xue. The author of this collection states that all the lyrics Liu sang were actually written by "the leading talents of the day." Yet access to formal education would not have been necessary to create these affecting texts in energetic vernacular language.

Zhou Dehua (ninth century) was a Zhejiangese singer believed to be daughter of Liu Caichun and her husband (see above). The one extant poem attributed to her appears in several Ming dynasty collections; the *Complete Tang Poems,* however, records it (in a slightly different version) as the work of the male poet Liu Yuxi (772–842).

Yan Lingbin (fl. before 881) was a high-class courtesan of Chang'an in the period before rebel forces under Huang Chao temporarily seized the capital. Known for her romantic and aesthetic nature, she was a fine calligrapher and collected poems given her by gallants.

Wang Susu (fl. before 881) lived in the same time and place as the previous poet. According to Sun Qi's nostalgic record of the capital's courtesans, she was skilled at banter.

Women of Religion

Qi Xiaoyao (dates unknown): The person behind the one poem recorded under her name is elusive: Is her biography fact, hagiographic glorification, or a mix? Certainly, her figure represents Tang women who pursued an ascetic life within Shangqing Taoism. Even her personal name suggests the transcendental roving possible for an advanced adept.

Li Ye *aka* **Li Jilan** (d. 784?): As a member of the group of writers around the influential poet, theorist-critic, and Buddhist monk Jiaoran (730–799), Li was active in the literary community of the lower Chang Jiang region. She wrote in a variety of forms, making confident use of tonally-regulated verse. It was likely on the basis of her reputation as a writer that Li was summoned north to enter the imperial household, although she returned home after a month or so. Allegedly, she wrote, during a military uprising, a poem believed to show support for the would-be ursurper and was executed for treason when Li Gua (Dezong, r. 779–805) regained the throne. Today only sixteen complete poems reliably attributed to this fine poet remain. Li is consistently identified as a Lady of the Tao; she seems also to have supported herself as a courtesan-*musicienne*.

Zhuo Yingying (fl. e. ninth century): A native of Chengdu, this poet became a lady of the imperial household. The editors of the *Complete Tang Poems* placed her in the section for "female transcendents" because of her literary association with the following poet, a dedicated Taoist ascetic; I follow their lead. They recorded four poems under Zhuo's name, one of which—"Spring View of Chengdu, the Brocade City"—is also attributed to Xue Tao.

Lu [*or* **Hu**] **Meiniang** *aka* **Lu Xiaoyao** (b. 792): This poet's given name—"Dame Eyebrows"—reflects her striking appearance. In 805, she was sent to enter the imperial harem during the five-month reign of Li Song (Xunzong), who'd been disabled by a stroke. Already known for her intellect and her skill as a maker of religious art, the poet soon heightened her reputation for spiritual inclinations; she ate little, in the manner of serious Taoist practitioners. The next emperor allowed Lu to take holy orders as a Lady of the Tao and return home to the far south, where she continued her mystic disciplines. It is reported that after her death, her coffin was discovered to be empty—a sign of transcendence realized—and that she was thereafter occasionally seen riding one of the purple clouds favored by holy spirits.

Yu Xuanji (844?–868?) The relatively large number of surviving poems from Yu's short life—around fifty—suggests the value that intervening generations found in them. She grew up a commoner in glittering Chang'an. In her mid-teens, she became concubine of an official who took her south and eventually dropped her. Yu entered a Taoist convent with connections to the imperial family and also supported herself as a courtesan—but the order of all these events is unclear. Then there is the mystery of her early death: A story written not long afterward states that she was executed for murdering her maid in a jealous rage, but doubts have been expressed regarding both the execution and her guilt.

Yuan Chun (fl. before 875), a "Female Scholar of the Tao," was evidently summoned to the Tang court from her home in Luoyang, in north central China. Fragments of lost poems by Yuan bear titles indicating literary exchanges with other women.

Haiyin (fl. l. ninth–e. tenth century) Having become a Buddhist nun in her youth, Haiyin resided in Guangci temple in Chengdu. Although she resisted fame, she became known for her pure and lofty intelligence, as well as the quality of her poetry. Only one poem survives.

Works Consulted

Birrell, Anne. 1986. *New Songs from a Jade Terrace: An Anthology of Early Chinese Love Poetry.* Harmondsworth & New York: Penguin.

____. 2004. *Games Poets Play: Readings in Medieval Chinese Poetry.* Cambridge: McGuiness.

Cahill, Suzanne E. 1986. "Performers and Female Taoist Adepts: Hsi Wang Mu as the Patron Saint of Women in Medieval China," *Journal of the American Oriental Society* 106: 155–68.

____. 1993. *Transcendence and Divine Passion: The Queen Mother of the West in Medieval China.* Stanford: Stanford University Press.

____. 2003. "Discipline and Transformation: Body and Practice in the Lives of Daoist Holy Women of Tang China." In *Women and Confucian Cultures in Premodern China, Korea, and Japan,* ed. Dorothy Ko, Jahyun Kim Haboush, and Joan R. Piggott. Berkeley: University of California Press.

Cao Yin et al., comp. pref. 1707. *Quan Tangshi.* Reprint, Taipei: Wenshije, 1978.

Chang, Kang-i Sun and Haun Saussy, eds. 1999. *Women Writers of Traditional China: An Anthology of Poetry and Criticism.* Stanford: Stanford University Press.

Chang, Kang-i Sun. 1997. "Ming and Qing Anthologies of Women's Poetry and their Selection Strategies." In *Writing Women in Late Imperial China,* ed. Ellen Widmer and Kang-I Sun Chang. Stanford: Stanford University Press.

Chen Dongyuan. 1928. *Zhongguo fun, shenghuo shi.* Reprint, Taipei, Shangwu, 1977.

Chen, Fan-pen. 1990-91. "Problems of Chinese Historiography As Seen in the Official Records on Yang Kuei-fei," *T'ang Studies* VII/IX: 83–96.

Eberhard, Wolfram. 1968. *The Local Cultures of South and East China.* Leiden: E. J. Brill.

Grant, Beata. 2003. *Daughters of Emptiness: Poems of Chinese Buddhist Nuns.* Boston: Wisdom Publications.

_____ & Wilt Idema. 2004. *The Red Brush: Writing Women of Imperial China.* Cambridge: Harvard University Asia Center.

Hucker, Charles O. 1985. *A Dictionary of Official Titles in Imperial China.* Stanford: Stanford University Press.

Karashima Tetsuji. 1964. *Gyō Genki Setsu To.* Kanshi taike 16. Tokyo: Dai Nihon.

Karetzky, Patricia. 1999. "The Representation of Women in Medieval China: Recent Archaeological Evidence," *T'ang Studies* XVII: 213–244.

Kondo Haruo. 1978. *Chūgoku gakugei daijiten.* Tokyo: Oshukan.

Kroll, Paul. 1987. "Basic Data on Reign-Dates and Local Government," *T'ang Studies* V: 95–104.

_____. 1990-91. "Po Chü-i's 'Song of Lasting Regret': A New Translation," *T'ang Studies* VIII–IX: 97–105.

_____. 2001. "Poetry of the T'ang Dynasty." In *The Columbia History of Chinese Literature*, ed. Victor H. Mair. New York: Columbia University Press.

Larsen, Jeanne. 1983. *The Chinese Poet Xue Tao: The Life and Works of a Mid-Tang Woman.* PhD dissertation, The University of Iowa.

_____, trans. 1987. *Brocade River Poems: Selected Works of the Tang Dynasty Courtesan Xue Tao.* Princeton: Lockert Library of Poetry in Translation, Princeton University Press.

Levy, Howard S. 1962a. "T'ang Courtesans, Ladies and Concubines," *Orient/West* VII (7): 49–64.

_____. 1962b. "The Gay Quarters of Ch'ang-an," *Orient/West* VII (9): 93–105.

_____. 1963 & 1964. "Record of the Gay Quarters," *Orient/West* VIII (5): 121–128; *Orient/West* VIII (6): 115–122; *Orient/West* IX (1): 103–110.

_____. 1964. "T'ang Women of Pleasure," *Sinologica* VIII, 2: 89–114.

McCraw, David. "Women and Old Chinese Poetry." unpublished partial draft monograph.

Mair, Victor, ed. 1994. *The Columbia Anthology of Traditional Chinese Literature*. New York: Columbia University Press.

Minford, John and Joseph S. M. Lau, eds. 2000. *Classical Chinese Literature: An Anthology of Translations, Vol. I*. New York: Columbia University Press.

Morohashi Tetsuji, ed-in-chief. 1957–60. *Dai Kan-Wa jiten*. 13 vols. Tokyo: Taishūkan shoten.

Nienhauser, William H. Jr., ed. 1986. *The Indiana Companion to Traditional Chinese Literature*. Bloomington: Indiana University Press.

Owen, Stephen. 1977. *The Poetry of the Early Tang*. New Haven: Yale University Press.

_____. 1995. "The Formation of the Tang Estate Poem," *Harvard Journal of Asiatic Studies* LV: 39–59.

_____. 1996. *An Anthology of Chinese Literature: Beginnings to 1911*. New York and London: W.W. Norton.

Robertson, Maureen. n.d. "Li Chi-lan." unpublished draft essay.

_____. 1992. "Refiguring the Feminine: Constructions of the Gendered Subject in Lyric Poetry by Women of Medieval and Late Imperial China." *Late Imperial China*, 13, no. 1.

_____. 1997. "Changing the Subject: Gender and Self-inscription in Authors' Prefaces and *Shi* Poetry." In *Writing Women in Late Imperial China*, ed. Ellen Widmer and Kang-I Sun Chang. Stanford: Stanford University Press.

Schafer, Edward. 1967. *The Vermilion Bird: T'ang Images of the South*. Berkeley: University of California Press.

_____. 1977. *Pacing the Void: T'ang Approaches to the Stars*. Berkeley: University of California Press.

____. 1978. "The Capeline Cantos: Verses on the Divine Loves of Taoist Priestesses," *Asiatische Studien* 32: 5-65.

____. 1979. "Three Divine Women of South China," *CLEAR (Chinese Literature: Essays, Articles, Reviews)* I: 31–42.

Shields, Anna M. 1997–98. "Gathering the 'Flowers' of Poetry and Song: An Analysis of Three Anthologies from the Late Tang and Shu," *T'ang Studies* XV/XVI: 1–40.

Stimson, Hugh M. 1976. *T'ang Poetic Vocabulary*. New Haven: Far Eastern Publications, Yale University.

Su Difei et al., eds. 1983. *Tangshi jianshang cidian*. Shanghai: Shanghai cishu chubanshe.

Su Zhezong. 1987. *Zhongguo lidai funü zuopin xuan*. Shanghai: Guji chubanshe.

Sun Qi. 1968. *Beili zhi*. In *Tangdai zongshu*, ed. Wang Wen'gao & Zhao Xizeng. Taipei: Xinxing.

Tan Zhengbi. 1930. *Zhongguo nüxingde wenxue shenghuo*. Taipei: Huluo, 1977.

____. 1934. *Zhongguo wenxuejia dacidian*. Shanghai: Shanghai shudian, 1981.

Twitchett, Denis, ed. 1979. *The Cambridge History of China, Vol. III: Sui and T'ang China, 589–906, Part I*. Cambridge: Harvard University Press.

Wagner, Marsha. 1984. *The Lotus Boat: The Origins of Tz'u Poetry in T'ang Popular Culture*. New York: Columbia University Press.

Walls, Jan Wilson. 1972. *The Poetry of Yu Hsüan-chi: A Translation, Annotation, Commentary and Critique*. PhD dissertation, Indiana University.

Wilhelm, Hellmut & David R. Knechtges. 1987. "T'ang T'ai-tsung's Poetry," *Tang Studies* V: 1–23.

Young, David & Jiann I. Lin, trans. 1998. *The Clouds Float North: The Complete Poems of Yu Xuanji*. Hanover and London: Wesleyan University Press.

Yuan Jie, Yin Fan et al., eds. 1958. *Tangren xuan Tangshi*. Hong Kong: Zhonghua shuju chubanshe.

Zhang Gongchang. 1975. *Zhongguo de jinü yu wenxue*. Taipei: Changshunshu shufang.

Zhang Huijuan. 1978. *Tangdai nüshiren yanjiu*. M.A. thesis, Zhongguo wenhua xüeyuan.

Zhang Pengzhou. 1981. *Xue Tao shijian*. Chengdu: Sichuan renmin chubanshe.

Zhang Qiyun et al., eds. 1962–68. *Zhongwen da cidian*. Yangmingshan: Zhongguo wenhua yanjiu suo.

Zhang Zhang and Huang She, eds. 1986. *Quan Tang-wudai ci*. Shanghai: Shanghai guji chubanshe.

Zheng Guangyi, ed-in-chief. 1991. *Zhongguo lidai cainü jianshang cidian*. Beijing: Zhongguo gongren chubanshe.

Zhou Xunchu, ed-in-chief. 1990. *Tangshi da cidian*. Shanghai: Jiangsu guji chubanshe.

Acknowledgments

Several of these translations have appeared, some in earlier versions, in *Artful Dodge, Circumference, Cold Mountain Review, Delos, Faultline, Hollins* magazine, *The Literary Review, Shenandoah,* and *Southern Poetry Review.* The editors of such journals deserve more praise than they get. Thank you.

The prose statements by Chinese anthologists quoted in the introduction were translated by Haun Saussy (for Wang Duanshu), Irving Yucheng Lo (for Luo Qilan), and Judith T. Zeitlin (for You Tong); I am most grateful for the work of these and other Sinologists. Complete English texts for Wang, Luo, and You appear in the groundbreaking *Women Writers of Traditional China.*

I am also indebted to the American Council of Learned Societies for an ACLS/Mellon Chinese Language Study Fellowship that allowed me to read some of the court women's poems with talented teachers at the Inter-University Program for Chinese Language Studies, then located in Taipei.

Heartfelt thanks to the National Endowment for the Arts for a Fellowship in Literary Translation and to Hollins University for sabbatical leave.

Friends and colleagues in Hollins' Faculty Writing Workshop and the Southeastern Chinese Literature and Art Circle responded helpfully to papers including drafts of some of these poems. Thanks, as well, to Kang-i Sun Chang, Cynthia Chennault, David Hinton, Victor Mair, J. P. Seaton, and Kam-ming Wong for encouragement at various points along the way. And to my teachers, from David Young at Oberlin and Chang T'ai-p'ing and Chih-p'ing Chou at Tunghai University, to W. South Coblin and, especially, Maureen Robertson at the University of Iowa, I offer appreciation for opening a most wonderful door. None of these people could possibly be blamed for my errors, but each of them has my deep gratitude.

About the Translator

Tang poetry called Jeanne Larsen to learn Chinese. In the early seventies, she spent two years in Taichung, Taiwan, on an Oberlin-Shansi fellowship, studying Mandarin and slowly reading poems in literary Chinese. She continued her studies at Oberlin, the University of Iowa (where she took her PhD in Comparative Literature), and Nagasaki University in Japan, later returning to Taiwan for intensive work at the Inter-University Center for Chinese Language Studies, then located at National Taiwan University. After her first book of her own poetry, she published *Brocade River Poems: Selected Works of the Tang Dynasty Courtesan Xue Tao*.

The author of three acclaimed novels set in historical China (*Silk Road, Bronze Mirror*, and *Manchu Palaces*), Jeanne Larsen has received numerous grants and awards for her writing. Her poems, translated poems, short fiction, and creative nonfiction have appeared in many literary quarterlies, and she has published scholarly articles on both Chinese and U.S. poetry. Professor of English at Hollins University, she is director of the highly-regarded graduate program in Creative Writing. She lives with her husband in the Roanoke Valley, between the Blue Ridge and the Appalachian highlands.

The Lannan Translations Selection Series

Ljuba Merlina Bortolani, *The Siege*

Olga Orozco, *Engravings Torn from Insomnia*

Gérard Martin, *The Hiddenness of the World*

Fadhil Al-Azzawi, *Miracle Maker*

Sándor Csoóri, *Before and After the Fall: New Poems*

Francisca Aguirre, *Ithaca*

Jean-Michel Maulpoix, *A Matter of Blue*

Willow, Wine, Mirror, Moon: Women's Poems from Tang China

For more on the Lannan Translations Selection Series
visit our Web site:
www.boaeditions.org

Printed in the USA
CPSIA information can be obtained
at www.ICGtesting.com
LVHW091516080824
787695LV00001B/144

9 781929 918744